LaTeX Reference Manual

A catalogue record for this book is available from the Hong Kong Public Libraries.

Published by Samurai Media Limited.

Email: info@samuraimedia.org

ISBN 978-988-14436-1-8

Background Cover Image by https://www.flickr.com/people/webtreatsetc/

Short Contents

Table of Contents

LaTeX2e: An unofficial reference manual

This document is an unofficial reference manual (version of May 2015) for LaTeX2e, a document preparation system.

1 About this document

This is an unofficial reference manual for the LaTeX2e document preparation system, which is a macro package for the TeX typesetting program (see Chapter 2 [Overview], page 3). This document's home page is http://home.gna.org/latexrefman. That page has links to the current output in various formats, sources, mailing list archives and subscriptions, and other infrastructure.

In this document, we will mostly just use 'LaTeX' rather than 'LaTeX2e', since the previous version of LaTeX (2.09) was retired many years ago.

LaTeX is currently maintained by a group of volunteers (http://latex-project.org). The official documentation written by the LaTeX project is available from their web site. This document is completely unofficial and has not been reviewed by the LaTeX maintainers. Do not send bug reports or anything else about this document to them. Instead, please send all comments to latexrefman-discuss@gna.org.

This document is a reference. There is a vast array of other sources of information about LaTeX, at all levels. Here are a few introductions.

http://ctan.org/pkg/latex-doc-ptr
> Two pages of recommended references to LaTeX documentation.

http://ctan.org/pkg/first-latex-doc
> Writing your first document, with a bit of both text and math.

http://ctan.org/pkg/usrguide
> The guide for document authors that is maintained as part of LaTeX; there are plenty of others available elsewhere.

http://ctan.org/pkg/lshort
> A short introduction to LaTeX, translated to many languages.

http://tug.org/begin.html
> Introduction to the TeX system, including LaTeX, with further references.

2 Overview of LaTeX

LaTeX is a system for typesetting documents. It was originally created by Leslie Lamport and is now maintained by a group of volunteers (`http://latex-project.org`). It is widely used, particularly for complex and technical documents, such as those involving mathematics.

A LaTeX user writes an input file containing text along with interspersed commands, for instance commands describing how the text should be formatted. It is implemented as a set of related commands that interface with Donald E. Knuth's TeX typesetting program (the technical term is that LaTeX is a *macro package* for the TeX engine). The user produces the output document by giving that file to the TeX engine.

The term LaTeX is also sometimes used to mean the language in which the document is marked up, that is, to mean the set of commands available to a LaTeX user.

The name LaTeX is short for "Lamport TeX". It is pronounced LAH-teck or LAY-teck, or sometimes LAY-tecks. Inside a document, produce the logo with `\LaTeX`. Where use of the logo is not sensible, such as in plain text, write it as 'LaTeX'.

2.1 Starting and ending

LaTeX files have a simple global structure, with a standard starting and ending. Here is a "hello, world" example:

```
\documentclass{article}
\begin{document}
Hello, \LaTeX\ world.
\end{document}
```

Here, the 'article' is the so-called *document class*, implemented in a file `article.cls`. Any document class can be used. A few document classes are defined by LaTeX itself, and vast array of others are widely available. See Chapter 3 [Document classes], page 6.

You can include other LaTeX commands between the `\documentclass` and the `\begin{document}` commands. This area is called the *preamble*.

The `\begin{document}` ... `\end{document}` is a so-called *environment*; the 'document' environment (and no others) is required in all LaTeX documents. LaTeX provides many environments itself, and many more are defined separately. See Chapter 8 [Environments], page 17.

The following sections discuss how to produce PDF or other output from a LaTeX input file.

2.2 Output files

LaTeX produces a main output file and at least two accessory files. The main output file's name ends in either `.dvi` or `.pdf`.

`.dvi`   If LaTeX is invoked with the system command `latex` then it produces a DeVice Independent file, with extension `.dvi`. You can view this file with a command such as `xdvi`, or convert it to a PostScript `.ps` file with `dvips` or to a Portable Document Format `.pdf` file with `dvipdfmx`. The contents of the file can be dumped in human-readable form with `dvitype`. A vast array of other DVI utility programs are available (`http://mirror.ctan.org/tex-archive/dviware`).

.pdf   If LaTeX is invoked via the system command `pdflatex`, among other commands (see Section 2.3 [TeX engines], page 4), then the main output is a Portable Document Format (PDF) file. Typically this is a self-contained file, with all fonts and images included.

LaTeX also produces at least two additional files.

.log   This transcript file contains summary information such as a list of loaded packages. It also includes diagnostic messages and perhaps additional information for any errors.

.aux   Auxiliary information is used by LaTeX for things such as cross references. For example, the first time that LaTeX finds a forward reference—a cross reference to something that has not yet appeared in the source—it will appear in the output as a doubled question mark `??`. When the referred-to spot does eventually appear in the source then LaTeX writes its location information to this `.aux` file. On the next invocation, LaTeX reads the location information from this file and uses it to resolve the reference, replacing the double question mark with the remembered location.

LaTeX may produce yet more files, characterized by the filename ending. These include a `.lof` file that is used to make a list of figures, a `.lot` file used to make a list of tables, and a `.toc` file used to make a table of contents. A particular class may create others; the list is open-ended.

2.3 TeX engines

LaTeX is defined to be a set of commands that are run by a TeX implementation (see Chapter 2 [Overview], page 3). This section gives a terse overview of the main programs.

latex
pdflatex   In TeX Live (`http://tug.org/texlive`, if LaTeX is invoked via either the system command `latex` or `pdflatex`, then the pdfTeX engine is run (`http://ctan.org/pkg/pdftex`). When invoked as `latex`, the main output is a `.dvi` file; as `pdflatex`, the main output is a `.pdf` file.

pdfTeX incorporates the e-TeX extensions to Knuth's original program (`http://ctan.org/pkg/etex`), including additional programming features and bi-directional typesetting, and has plenty of extensions of its own. e-TeX is available on its own as the command `etex`, but this is plain TeX (and produces `.dvi`).

In other TeX distributions, `latex` may invoke e-TeX rather than pdfTeX. In any case, the e-TeX extensions can be assumed to be available in LaTeX.

lualatex   If LaTeX is invoked via the system command `lualatex`, the LuaTeX engine is run (`http://ctan.org/pkg/luatex`). This program allows code written in the scripting language Lua (`http://luatex.org`) to interact with TeX's typesetting. LuaTeX handles UTF-8 Unicode input natively, can handle Open-Type and TrueType fonts, and produces a `.pdf` file by default. There is also `dvilualatex` to produce a `.dvi` file, but this is rarely used.

xelatex   If LaTeX is invoked with the system command `xelatex`, the XeTeX engine is run (`http://tug.org/xetex`). Like LuaTeX, XeTeX also natively supports UTF-8 Unicode and TrueType and OpenType fonts, though the implementation is completely different, mainly using external libraries instead of internal code. XeTeX produces a `.pdf` file as output; it does not support DVI output.

Other variants of LaTeX and TeX exist, e.g., to provide additional support for Japanese and other languages ([u]pTeX, `http://ctan.org/pkg/ptex`, `http://ctan.org/pkg/uptex`).

2.4 LaTeX command syntax

In the LaTeX input file, a command name starts with a backslash character, `\`. The name itself then consists of either (a) a string of letters or (b) a single non-letter.

A command may be followed by zero, one, or more arguments, either required or optional. Required arguments are contained in curly braces, `{...}`. Optional arguments are contained in square brackets, `[...]`. Generally, but not universally, if the command accepts an optional argument, it comes first, before any required arguments.

Some commands have a `*` form that is related to the form without a `*`, such as `\chapter` and `\chapter*`.

LaTeX commands are case sensitive; neither `\Begin{document}` nor `\begin{Document}` will work. Most commands are lowercase, but in any event you must enter all commands in the same case as they are defined.

This manual describes all accepted options and `*`-forms for the commands it covers (barring unintentional omissions, a.k.a. bugs).

3 Document classes

The document's overall class is defined with this command, which is normally the first command in a LaTeX source file.

> `\documentclass[options]{class}`

The following document *class* names are built into LaTeX. (Many other document classes are available as separate packages; see Chapter 2 [Overview], page 3.)

article   For a journal article, a presentation, and miscellaneous general use.

book   Full-length books, including chapters and possibly including front matter, such as a preface, and back matter, such as an appendix (see Chapter 23 [Front/back matter], page 80).

report   For documents of length between an article and a book, such as technical reports or theses, which may contain several chapters.

slides   For slide presentations—rarely used today. In its place the beamer package is perhaps the most prevalent (see Section A.1 [beamer template], page 87).

Standard *options* are described in the next section.

3.1 Document class options

You can specify so-called *global options* or *class options* to the `\documentclass` command by enclosing them in square brackets. To specify more than one *option*, separate them with a comma, as in:

> `\documentclass[option1,option2,...]{class}`

Here is the list of the standard class options.

All of the standard classes except slides accept the following options for selecting the typeface size (default is 10pt):

> `10pt  11pt  12pt`

All of the standard classes accept these options for selecting the paper size (default is letterpaper):

> `a4paper a5paper b5paper executivepaper legalpaper letterpaper`

Miscellaneous other options:

draft
final   Mark (draft) or do not mark (final) overfull boxes with a black box in the margin; default is final.

fleqn   Put displayed formulas flush left; default is centered.

landscape
            Selects landscape format; default is portrait.

leqno   Put equation numbers on the left side of equations; default is the right side.

openbib   Use "open" bibliography format.

`titlepage`
`notitlepage`
> Specifies whether the title page is separate; default depends on the class.

The following options are not available with the `slides` class.

`onecolumn`
`twocolumn`
> Typeset in one or two columns; default is `onecolumn`.

`oneside`
`twoside`
> Selects one- or two-sided layout; default is `oneside`, except that in the `book` class the default is `twoside`.
>
> For one-sided printing, the text is centered on the page. For two-sided printing, the `\evensidemargin` (`\oddsidemargin`) parameter determines the distance on even (odd) numbered pages between the left side of the page and the text's left margin, with `\oddsidemargin` being 40% of the difference between `\paperwidth` and `\textwidth`, and `\evensidemargin` is the remainder.

`openright`
`openany`
> Determines if a chapter should start on a right-hand page; default is `openright` for `book`, and `openany` for `report`.

The `slides` class offers the option `clock` for printing the time at the bottom of each note.

Additional packages are loaded like this:

```
\usepackage[options]{pkg}
```

To specify more than one package, you can separate them with a comma, as in `\usepackage{pkg1,pkg2,...}`, or use multiple `\usepackage` commands.

Any options given in the `\documentclass` command that are unknown by the selected document class are passed on to the packages loaded with `\usepackage`.

4 Fonts

Two important aspects of selecting a *font* are specifying a size and a style. The LaTeX commands for doing this are described here.

4.1 Font styles

The following type style commands are supported by LaTeX.

This first group of commands is typically used with an argument, as in `\textit{italic text}`. In the table below, the corresponding command in parenthesis is the "declaration form", which takes no arguments. The scope of the declaration form lasts until the next type style command or the end of the current group.

These commands, in both the argument form and the declaration form, are cumulative; e.g., you can say either `\sffamily\bfseries` or `\bfseries\sffamily` to get bold sans serif.

You can alternatively use an environment form of the declarations; for instance, `\begin{ttfamily}...\end{ttfamily}`.

These font-switching commands automatically insert italic corrections if needed. (See Section 19.6 [\/], page 68, for the details of italic corrections.) Specifically, they insert the italic correction unless the following character is in the list `\nocorrlist`, which by default consists of a period and a comma. To suppress the automatic insertion of italic correction, use `\nocorr` at the start or end of the command argument, such as `\textit{\nocorr text}` or `\textsc{text \nocorr}`.

`\textrm (\rmfamily)`
        Roman.

`\textit (\itshape)`
        Italics.

`\emph`   Emphasis (switches between `\textit` and `\textrm`).

`\textmd (\mdseries)`
        Medium weight (default).

`\textbf (\bfseries)`
        Boldface.

`\textup (\upshape)`
        Upright (default). The opposite of slanted.

`\textsl (\slshape)`
        Slanted.

`\textsf (\sffamily)`
        Sans serif.

`\textsc (\scshape)`
        Small caps.

`\texttt (\ttfamily)`
        Typewriter.

`\textnormal (\normalfont)`
>   Main document font.

`\mathrm`   Roman, for use in math mode.

`\mathbf`   Boldface, for use in math mode.

`\mathsf`   Sans serif, for use in math mode.

`\mathtt`   Typewriter, for use in math mode.

`\mathit`
`(\mit)`   Italics, for use in math mode.

`\mathnormal`
>   For use in math mode, e.g. inside another type style declaration.

`\mathcal`   'Calligraphic' letters, for use in math mode.

In addition, the command `\mathversion{bold}` can be used for switching to bold letters and symbols in formulas. `\mathversion{normal}` restores the default.

Finally, the command `\oldstylenums{`*numerals*`}` will typeset so-called "old-style" numerals, which have differing heights and depths (and sometimes widths) from the standard "lining" numerals. LaTeX's default fonts support this, and will respect `\textbf` (but not other styles; there are no italic old-style numerals in Computer Modern). Many other fonts have old-style numerals also; sometimes the `textcomp` package must be loaded, and sometimes package options are provided to make them the default. FAQ entry: `http://www.tex.ac.uk/cgi-bin/texfaq2html?label=osf`.

LaTeX also provides the following commands, which unconditionally switch to the given style, that is, are *not* cumulative. Also, they are used differently than the above commands: `{\`*cmd* `...}` instead of `\`*cmd*`{...}`. These are two unrelated constructs.

`\bf`   Switch to **bold face**.

`\cal`   Switch to calligraphic letters for math.

`\em`   Emphasis (italics within roman, roman within italics).

`\it`   Italics.

`\rm`   Roman.

`\sc`   Small caps.

`\sf`   Sans serif.

`\sl`   Slanted (oblique).

`\tt`   Typewriter (monospace, fixed-width).

Some people consider the unconditional font-switching commands, such as `\tt`, obsolete and *only* the cumulative commands (`\texttt`) should be used. I (Karl) do not agree. There are perfectly reasonable situations when an unconditional font switch is precisely what you need to get the desired output; for one example, see Section 8.4 [`description`], page 18. Both sets of commands have their place.

4.2 Font sizes

The following standard type size commands are supported by LaTeX. The table shows the command name and the corresponding actual font size used (in points) with the '10pt', '11pt', and '12pt' document size options, respectively (see Section 3.1 [Document class options], page 6).

Command	10pt	11pt	12pt
\tiny	5	6	6
\scriptsize	7	8	8
\footnotesize	8	9	10
\small	9	10	10.95
\normalsize (default)	10	10.95	12
\large	12	12	14.4
\Large	14.4	14.4	17.28
\LARGE	17.28	17.28	20.74
\huge	20.74	20.74	24.88
\Huge	24.88	24.88	24.88

The commands as listed here are "declaration forms". The scope of the declaration form lasts until the next type style command or the end of the current group. You can also use the environment form of these commands; for instance, \begin{tiny}...\end{tiny}.

4.3 Low-level font commands

These commands are primarily intended for writers of macros and packages. The commands listed here are only a subset of the available ones.

\fontencoding{enc}
>   Select font encoding. Valid encodings include OT1 and T1.

\fontfamily{family}
>   Select font family. Valid families include:
>   - cmr for Computer Modern Roman
>   - cmss for Computer Modern Sans Serif
>   - cmtt for Computer Modern Typewriter
>
>   and numerous others.

\fontseries{series}
>   Select font series. Valid series include:
>   - m Medium (normal)
>   - b Bold
>   - c Condensed
>   - bc Bold condensed
>   - bx Bold extended
>
>   and various other combinations.

\fontshape{shape}
>   Select font shape. Valid shapes are:

- n Upright (normal)
- it Italic
- sl Slanted (oblique)
- sc Small caps
- ui Upright italics
- ol Outline

The two last shapes are not available for most font families.

`\fontsize{size}{skip}`

Set font size. The first parameter is the font size to switch to and the second is the line spacing to use; this is stored in a parameter named `\baselineskip`. The unit of both parameters defaults to pt. The default `\baselineskip` for the Computer Modern typeface is 1.2 times the `\fontsize`.

The line spacing is also multiplied by the value of the `\baselinestretch` parameter when the type size changes; the default is 1. However, the best way to "double space" a document, if you should be unlucky enough to have to produce such, is to use the setspace package; see `http://www.tex.ac.uk/cgi-bin/texfaq2html?label=linespace`.

`\linespread{factor}`

Equivalent to `\renewcommand{\baselinestretch}{factor}`, and therefore must be followed by `\selectfont` to have any effect. Best specified in the preamble, or use the setspace package, as described just above.

The changes made by calling the font commands described above do not come into effect until `\selectfont` is called.

`\usefont{enc}{family}{series}{shape}`

The same as invoking `\fontencoding`, `\fontfamily`, `\fontseries` and `\fontshape` with the given parameters, followed by `\selectfont`.

5 Layout

Miscellaneous commands for controlling the general layout of the page.

5.1 \onecolumn

The \onecolumn declaration starts a new page and produces single-column output. This is the default.

5.2 \twocolumn

Synopsis:

> \twocolumn[*text1col*]

The \twocolumn declaration starts a new page and produces two-column output. If the optional *text1col* argument is present, it is typeset in one-column mode before the two-column typesetting starts.

These parameters control typesetting in two-column output:

\columnsep

> The distance between columns (35pt by default).

\columnseprule

> The width of the rule between columns; the default is 0pt, so there is no rule.

\columnwidth

> The width of the current column; this is equal to \textwidth in single-column text.

These parameters control float behavior in two-column output:

\dbltopfraction

> Maximum fraction at the top of a two-column page that may be occupied by floats. Default '.7', can be usefully redefined to (say) '.9' to avoid going to float pages so soon.

\dblfloatpagefraction

> The minimum fraction of a float page that must be occupied by floats, for a two-column float page. Default '.5'.

\dblfloatsep

> Distance between floats at the top or bottom of a two-column float page. Default '12pt plus2pt minus2pt' for '10pt' and '11pt' documents, '14pt plus2pt minus4pt' for '12pt'.

\dbltextfloatsep

> Distance between a multi-column float at the top or bottom of a page and the main text. Default '20pt plus2pt minus4pt'.

5.3 \flushbottom

The \flushbottom declaration makes all text pages the same height, adding extra vertical space where necessary to fill out the page.

This is the default if twocolumn mode is selected (see Section 3.1 [Document class options], page 6).

5.4 \raggedbottom

The \raggedbottom declaration makes all pages the natural height of the material on that page. No rubber lengths will be stretched.

5.5 Page layout parameters

\headheight

Height of the box that contains the running head. Default is '30pt', except in the book class, where it varies with the type size.

\headsep   Vertical distance between the bottom of the header line and the top of the main text. Default is '25pt', except in the book class, where it varies with the type size.

\footskip

Distance from the baseline of the last line of text to the baseline of the page footer. Default is '30pt', except in the book class, where it varies with the type size.

\linewidth

Width of the current line, decreased for each nested list (see Section 8.16 [list], page 25). Specifically, it is smaller than \textwidth by the sum of \leftmargin and \rightmargin (see Section 8.14 [itemize], page 23). The default varies with the font size, paper width, two-column mode, etc. For an article document in '10pt', it's set to '345pt'; in two-column mode, that becomes '229.5pt'.

\textheight

The normal vertical height of the page body; the default varies with the font size, document class, etc. For an article or report document in '10pt', it's set to '43\baselineskip'; for book, it's '41\baselineskip'. For '11pt', it's '38\baselineskip' and for '12pt', '36\baselineskip'.

\textwidth

The full horizontal width of the entire page body; the default varies as usual. For an article or report document, it's '345pt' at '10pt', '360pt' at '11pt', and '390pt' at '12pt'. For a book document, it's '4.5in' at '10pt', and '5in' at '11pt' or '12pt'.

In multi-column output, \textwidth remains the width of the entire page body, while \columnwidth is the width of one column (see Section 5.2 [\twocolumn], page 12).

In lists (see Section 8.16 [list], page 25), \textwidth remains the width of the entire page body (and \columnwidth the width of the entire column), while \linewidth may decrease for nested lists.

Inside a minipage (see Section 8.18 [minipage], page 26) or `\parbox` (see Section 20.5 [\parbox], page 71), all the width-related parameters are set to the specified width, and revert to their normal values at the end of the `minipage` or `\parbox`.

For completeness: `\hsize` is the TeX primitive parameter used when text is broken into lines. It should not be used in normal LaTeX documents.

`\topmargin`

Space between the top of the TeX page (one inch from the top of the paper, by default) and the top of the header. The default is computed based on many other parameters: `\paperheight` − `2in` − `\headheight` − `\headsep` − `\textheight` − `\footskip`, and then divided by two.

`\topskip` Minimum distance between the top of the page body and the baseline of the first line of text. For the standard classes, the default is the same as the font size, e.g., '10pt' at '10pt'.

6 Sectioning

Sectioning commands provide the means to structure your text into units:

`\part`

`\chapter`   (`report` and `book` class only)

`\section`

`\subsection`
`\subsubsection`
`\paragraph`
`\subparagraph`

All sectioning commands take the same general form, e.g.,

> `\chapter[`*`toctitle`*`]{`*`title`*`}`

In addition to providing the heading *title* in the main text, the section title can appear in two other places:

1. The table of contents.
2. The running head at the top of the page.

You may not want the same text in these places as in the main text. To handle this, the sectioning commands have an optional argument *toctitle* that, when given, specifies the text for these other places.

Also, all sectioning commands have *-forms that print *title* as usual, but do not include a number and do not make an entry in the table of contents. For instance:

> `\section*{Preamble}`

The `\appendix` command changes the way following sectional units are numbered. The `\appendix` command itself generates no text and does not affect the numbering of parts. The normal use of this command is something like

> `\chapter{A Chapter}`
>
> `...`
>
> `\appendix`
> `\chapter{The First Appendix}`

The `secnumdepth` counter controls printing of section numbers. The setting

> `\setcounter{secnumdepth}{`*`level`*`}`

suppresses heading numbers at any depth $>$ *level*, where `chapter` is level zero. (See Section 13.4 [\setcounter], page 47.)

7 Cross references

One reason for numbering things like figures and equations is to refer the reader to them, as in "See Figure 3 for more details."

7.1 \label

Synopsis:

> \label{*key*}

A \label command appearing in ordinary text assigns to *key* the number of the current sectional unit; one appearing inside a numbered environment assigns that number to *key*.

A *key* name can consist of any sequence of letters, digits, or punctuation characters. Upper and lowercase letters are distinguished, as usual.

To avoid accidentally creating two labels with the same name, it is common to use labels consisting of a prefix and a suffix separated by a colon or period. Some conventionally-used prefixes:

ch   for chapters

sec   for lower-level sectioning commands

fig   for figures

tab   for tables

eq   for equations

Thus, a label for a figure would look like `fig:snark` or `fig.snark`.

7.2 \pageref{*key*}

Synopsis:

> \pageref{*key*}

The \pageref{*key*} command produces the page number of the place in the text where the corresponding \label{*key*} command appears.

7.3 \ref{*key*}

Synopsis:

> \ref{*key*}

The \ref command produces the number of the sectional unit, equation, footnote, figure, ..., of the corresponding \label command (see Section 7.1 [\label], page 16). It does not produce any text, such as the word 'Section' or 'Figure', just the bare number itself.

8 Environments

LaTeX provides many environments for marking off certain text. Each environment begins and ends in the same manner:

```
\begin{envname}
...
\end{envname}
```

8.1 abstract

Synopsis:

```
\begin{abstract}
...
\end{abstract}
```

Environment for producing an abstract, possibly of multiple paragraphs.

8.2 array

Synopsis:

```
\begin{array}{template}
col1 text &col2 text ... &coln text \\
...
\end{array}
```

Math arrays are produced with the `array` environment, normally within an `equation` environment (see Section 8.9 [equation], page 20). It has a single mandatory *template* argument describing the number of columns and the alignment within them. Each column *col* is specified by a single letter that tells how items in each row of that column should be formatted, as follows:

c   centered

l   flush left

r   flush right

Column entries are separated by &. Column entries may include other LaTeX commands. Each row of the array is terminated with \\.

In the template, the construct @{text} puts *text* between columns in each row.

Here's an example:

```
\begin{equation}
  \begin{array}{lrc}
  left1 & right1 & centered1 \\
  left2 & right2 & centered2 \\
  \end{array}
\end{equation}
```

The `\arraycolsep` parameter defines half the width of the space separating columns; the default is '5pt'. See Section 8.24 [tabular], page 32, for other parameters which affect formatting in `array` environments, namely `\arrayrulewidth` and `\arraystretch`.

The `array` environment can only be used in math mode.

8.3 center

Synopsis:

```
\begin{center}
line1 \\
line2 \\
\end{center}
```

The center environment allows you to create a paragraph consisting of lines that are centered within the left and right margins on the current page. Each line is terminated with the string \\.

8.3.1 \centering

The \centering declaration corresponds to the center environment. This declaration can be used inside an environment such as quote or in a parbox. Thus, the text of a figure or table can be centered on the page by putting a \centering command at the beginning of the figure or table environment.

Unlike the center environment, the \centering command does not start a new paragraph; it simply changes how LaTeX formats paragraph units. To affect a paragraph unit's format, the scope of the declaration must contain the blank line or \end command (of an environment such as quote) that ends the paragraph unit.

Here's an example:

```
\begin{quote}
\centering
first line \\
second line \\
\end{quote}
```

8.4 description

Synopsis:

```
\begin{description}
\item [label1] item1
\item [label2] item2
...
\end{description}
```

The description environment is used to make labelled lists. Each *label* is typeset in bold, flush right. The *item* text may contain multiple paragraphs.

Another variation: since the bold style is applied to the labels, if you typeset a label in typewriter using \texttt, you'll get bold typewriter: \item[\texttt{bold and typewriter}]. This may be too bold, among other issues. To get just typewriter, use \tt, which resets all other style variations: \item[{\tt plain typewriter}].

For details about list spacing, see Section 8.14 [itemize], page 23.

8.5 displaymath

Synopsis:

```
\begin{displaymath}
math
\end{displaymath}
```

or

```
\[math\]
```

The `displaymath` environment (`\[...\]` is a synonym) typesets the *math* text on its own line, centered by default. The global `fleqn` option makes equations flush left; see Section 3.1 [Document class options], page 6.

No equation number is added to `displaymath` text; to get an equation number, use the `equation` environment (see Section 8.9 [equation], page 20).

8.6 document

The `document` environment encloses the body of a document. It is required in every LATEX document. See Section 2.1 [Starting and ending], page 3.

8.7 enumerate

Synopsis:

```
\begin{enumerate}
\item item1
\item item2
  ...
\end{enumerate}
```

The `enumerate` environment produces a numbered list. Enumerations can be nested within one another, up to four levels deep. They can also be nested within other paragraph-making environments, such as `itemize` (see Section 8.14 [itemize], page 23) and `description` (see Section 8.4 [description], page 18).

Each item of an enumerated list begins with an `\item` command. There must be at least one `\item` command within the environment.

By default, the numbering at each level is done like this:

1. 1., 2., . . .
2. (a), (b), . . .
3. i., ii., . . .
4. A., B., . . .

The `enumerate` environment uses the counters `\enumi` through `\enumiv` counters (see Chapter 13 [Counters], page 46). If the optional argument to `\item` is given, the counter is not incremented for that item.

The `enumerate` environment uses the commands `\labelenumi` through `\labelenumiv` to produce the default label. So, you can use `\renewcommand` to change the labels (see Section 12.1 [\newcommand & \renewcommand], page 43). For instance, to have the first level use uppercase letters:

```
\renewcommand{\labelenumi}{\Alph{enumi}}
```

8.8 eqnarray

First, a caveat: the `eqnarray` environment has some infelicities which cannot be overcome; the article "Avoid eqnarray!" by Lars Madsen describes them in detail (`http://tug.org/TUGboat/tb33-1/tb103madsen.pdf`). The bottom line is that it is better to use the `align` environment (and others) from the `amsmath` package.

Nevertheless, here is a description of `eqnarray`:

```
\begin{eqnarray}   (or eqnarray*)
formula1 \\
formula2 \\
...
\end{eqnarray}
```

The `eqnarray` environment is used to display a sequence of equations or inequalities. It is similar to a three-column `array` environment, with consecutive rows separated by \\ and consecutive items within a row separated by an &.

* can also be used to separate equations, with its normal meaning of not allowing a page break at that line.

An equation number is placed on every line unless that line has a \nonumber command. Alternatively, The *-form of the environment (\begin{eqnarray*} ... \end{eqnarray*}) will omit equation numbering entirely, while otherwise being the same as `eqnarray`.

The command \lefteqn is used for splitting long formulas across lines. It typesets its argument in display style flush left in a box of zero width.

8.9 equation

Synopsis:

```
\begin{equation}
math
\end{equation}
```

The `equation` environment starts a `displaymath` environment (see Section 8.5 [displaymath], page 19), e.g., centering the *math* text on the page, and also places an equation number in the right margin.

8.10 figure

```
\begin{figure[*]}[placement]
figbody
\label{label}
\caption[loftitle]{text}
\end{figure}
```

Figures are objects that are not part of the normal text, and are instead "floated" to a convenient place, such as the top of a page. Figures will not be split between two pages.

When typesetting in double-columns, the starred form produces a full-width figure (across both columns).

The optional argument *placement* determines where LaTeX will try to place your figure. There are four places where LaTeX can possibly put a float:

t   (Top)—at the top of a text page.

b   (Bottom)—at the bottom of a text page. However, b is not allowed for full-width floats (`figure*`) with double-column output. To ameliorate this, use the **stfloats** or dblfloatfix package, but see the discussion at caveats in the FAQ: `http://www.tex.ac.uk/cgi-bin/texfaq2html?label=2colfloat`.

h   (Here)—at the position in the text where the `figure` environment appears. However, t is not allowed by itself; t is automatically added.

            To absolutely force a figure to appear "here", you can `\usepackage{float}` and use the H specifier which it defines. For further discussion, see the FAQ entry at `http://www.tex.ac.uk/cgi-bin/texfaq2html?label=figurehere`.

p   (Page of floats)—on a separate float page, which is a page containing no text, only floats.

!   Used in addition to one of the above; for this float only, LaTeX ignores the restrictions on both the number of floats that can appear and the relative amounts of float and non-float text on the page. The ! specifier does *not* mean "put the float here"; see above.

The standard **report** and **article** classes use the default placement tbp.

The body of the figure is made up of whatever text, LaTeX commands, etc. you wish.

The `\caption` command specifies caption *text* for the figure. The caption is numbered by default. If *loftitle* is present, it is used in the list of figures instead of *text* (see Section 23.1 [Tables of contents], page 80).

Parameters relating to fractions of pages occupied by float and non-float text:

`\bottomfraction`

            The maximum fraction of the page allowed to be occupied by floats at the bottom; default '.3'.

`\floatpagefraction`

            The minimum fraction of a float page that must be occupied by floats; default '.5'.

`\textfraction`

            Minimum fraction of a page that must be text; if floats take up too much space to preserve this much text, floats will be moved to a different page. The default is '.2'.

`\topfraction`

            Maximum fraction at the top of a page that may be occupied before floats; default '.7'.

Parameters relating to vertical space around floats:

`\floatsep`

            Space between floats at the top or bottom of a page; default '12pt plus2pt minus2pt'.

`\intextsep`

> Space above and below a float in the middle of the main text; default '12pt plus2pt minus2pt' for '10pt' and '11pt' styles, '14pt plus4pt minus4pt' for '12pt'.

`\textfloatsep`

> Space between the last (first) float at the top (bottom) of a page; default '20pt plus2pt minus4pt'.

Counters relating to the number of floats on a page:

`bottomnumber`

> Maximum number of floats that can appear at the bottom of a text page; default 1.

`dbltopnumber`

> Maximum number of full-sized floats that can appear at the top of a two-column page; default 2.

`topnumber`

> Maximum number of floats that can appear at the top of a text page; default 2.

`totalnumber`

> Maximum number of floats that can appear on a text page; default 3.

The principal TeX FAQ entry relating to floats: `http://www.tex.ac.uk/cgi-bin/texfaq2html?label=floats`.

8.11 filecontents: Create external files

Synopsis:

```
\begin{filecontents}{filename}
contents-of-file
\end{filecontents}
...
\documentclass{my-document-class}
```

The `filecontents` environment is an *initial command*, meaning that it can be used only before the `\documentclass` command, as in the synopsis above.

LaTeX will create a file named *filename* with the content *contents-of-file* preceded by a header comment indicating how and when the file was generated. If the file already exists then nothing will happen.

You can also use the `filecontents` package, which has the following advantages:

- If the file already exists, then it will be overwritten.

- You can use the `filecontents` environment at any point after the declaration `\usepackage{filecontents}`, not just before `\documentclass`.

- The `filecontents` package also provides a `filecontents*` environment which is used in the same way as the `filecontents` environment except that it won't insert any leading comment, so it is better suited to create files which aren't in LaTeX format.

The `filecontents` environment only creates the file, and is unrelated to using the created file. So you need to use, for instance, `\input` or `\usepackage` or `\bibliography` or whatever is applicable, to use the created file.

This environment is also useful to make a document in a self-contained file, for example, for a bug report, or to keep the content of a `.bib` file in the same file as the main document.

8.12 flushleft

```
\begin{flushleft}
line1 \\
line2 \\
...
\end{flushleft}
```

The `flushleft` environment allows you to create a paragraph consisting of lines that are flush to the left-hand margin and ragged right Each line must be terminated with the string `\\`.

8.12.1 \raggedright

The `\raggedright` declaration corresponds to the `flushleft` environment. This declaration can be used inside an environment such as `quote` or in a `parbox`.

Unlike the `flushleft` environment, the `\raggedright` command does not start a new paragraph; it only changes how LaTeX formats paragraph units. To affect a paragraph unit's format, the scope of the declaration must contain the blank line or `\end` command that ends the paragraph unit.

8.13 flushright

```
\begin{flushright}
line1 \\
line2 \\
...
\end{flushright}
```

The `flushright` environment allows you to create a paragraph consisting of lines that are flush to the right-hand margin and ragged left. Each line must be terminated with the string `\\`.

8.13.1 \raggedleft

The `\raggedleft` declaration corresponds to the `flushright` environment. This declaration can be used inside an environment such as `quote` or in a `parbox`.

Unlike the `flushright` environment, the `\raggedleft` command does not start a new paragraph; it only changes how LaTeX formats paragraph units. To affect a paragraph unit's format, the scope of the declaration must contain the blank line or `\end` command that ends the paragraph unit.

8.14 itemize

Synopsis:

```
\begin{itemize}
\item item1
\item item2
...
\end{itemize}
```

The `itemize` environment produces an "unordered", "bulleted" list. Itemizations can be nested within one another, up to four levels deep. They can also be nested within other paragraph-making environments, such as **enumerate** (see Section 8.7 [enumerate], page 19).

Each item of an `itemize` list begins with an `\item` command. There must be at least one `\item` command within the environment.

By default, the marks at each level look like this:

1. • (bullet)

2. -- (bold en-dash)

3. * (asterisk)

4. · (centered dot)

The `itemize` environment uses the commands `\labelitemi` through `\labelitemiv` to produce the default label. So, you can use `\renewcommand` to change the labels. For instance, to have the first level use diamonds:

```
\renewcommand{\labelitemi}{$\diamond$}
```

The `\leftmargini` through `\leftmarginvi` parameters define the distance between the left margin of the enclosing environment and the left margin of the list. By convention, `\leftmargin` is set to the appropriate `\leftmarginN` when a new level of nesting is entered.

The defaults vary from '`.5em`' (highest levels of nesting) to '`2.5em`' (first level), and are a bit reduced in two-column mode. This example greatly reduces the margin space for outermost lists:

```
\setlength{\leftmargini}{1.25em} % default 2.5em
```

Some parameters that affect list formatting:

`\itemindent`
> Extra indentation before each item in a list; default zero.

`\labelsep`
> Space between the label and text of an item; default '`.5em`'.

`\labelwidth`
> Width of the label; default '`2em`', or '`1.5em`' in two-column mode.

`\listparindent`
> Extra indentation added to second and subsequent paragraphs within a list item; default '`0pt`'.

`\rightmargin`
> Horizontal distance between the right margin of the list and the enclosing environment; default '`0pt`', except in the **quote**, **quotation**, and **verse** environments, where it is set equal to `\leftmargin`.

Parameters affecting vertical spacing between list items (rather loose, by default).

`\itemsep`   Vertical space between items. The default is `2pt plus1pt minus1pt` for 10pt documents, `3pt plus2pt minus1pt` for 11pt, and `4.5pt plus2pt minus1pt` for 12pt.

`\parsep`   Extra vertical space between paragraphs within a list item. Defaults are the same as `\itemsep`.

`\topsep`   Vertical space between the first item and the preceding paragraph. For top-level lists, the default is `8pt plus2pt minus4pt` for 10pt documents, `9pt plus3pt minus5pt` for 11pt, and `10pt plus4pt minus6pt` for 12pt. These are reduced for nested lists.

`\partopsep`

Extra space added to `\topsep` when the list environment starts a paragraph. The default is `2pt plus1pt minus1pt` for 10pt documents, `3pt plus1pt minus1pt` for 11pt, and `3pt plus2pt minus2pt` for 12pt.

Especially for lists with short items, it may be desirable to elide space between items. Here is an example defining an `itemize*` environment with no extra spacing between items, or between paragraphs within a single item (`\parskip` is not list-specific, see Section 15.3 [\parskip], page 50):

```
\newenvironment{itemize*}%
  {\begin{itemize}%
    \setlength{\itemsep}{0pt}%
    \setlength{\parsep}{0pt}}%
    \setlength{\parskip}{0pt}}%
  {\end{itemize}}
```

8.15 `letter` environment: writing letters

This environment is used for creating letters. See Chapter 24 [Letters], page 82.

8.16 `list`

The `list` environment is a generic environment which is used for defining many of the more specific environments. It is seldom used in documents, but often in macros.

```
\begin{list}{labeling}{spacing}
\item item1
\item item2
...
\end{list}
```

The mandatory *labeling* argument specifies how items should be labelled (unless the optional argument is supplied to `\item`). This argument is a piece of text that is inserted in a box to form the label. It can and usually does contain other LaTeX commands.

The mandatory *spacing* argument contains commands to change the spacing parameters for the list. This argument will most often be empty, i.e., `{}`, which leaves the default spacing.

The width used for typesetting the list items is specified by `\linewidth` (see Section 5.5 [Page layout parameters], page 13).

8.17 math

Synopsis:

```
\begin{math}
math
\end{math}
```

The `math` environment inserts the given *math* within the running text. `\(...\)` and `$...$` are synonyms. See Chapter 16 [Math formulas], page 52.

8.18 minipage

```
\begin{minipage}[position][height][inner-pos]{width}
text
\end{minipage}
```

The `minipage` environment typesets its body *text* in a block that will not be broken across pages. This is similar to the `\parbox` command (see Section 20.5 [\parbox], page 71), but unlike `\parbox`, other paragraph-making environments can be used inside a minipage.

The arguments are the same as for `\parbox` (see Section 20.5 [\parbox], page 71).

By default, paragraphs are not indented in the `minipage` environment. You can restore indentation with a command such as `\setlength{\parindent}{1pc}` command.

Footnotes in a `minipage` environment are handled in a way that is particularly useful for putting footnotes in figures or tables. A `\footnote` or `\footnotetext` command puts the footnote at the bottom of the minipage instead of at the bottom of the page, and it uses the `\mpfootnote` counter instead of the ordinary `footnote` counter (see Chapter 13 [Counters], page 46).

However, don't put one minipage inside another if you are using footnotes; they may wind up at the bottom of the wrong minipage.

8.19 picture

```
\begin{picture}(width,height)(x offset,y offset)
... picture commands ...
\end{picture}
```

The `picture` environment allows you to create just about any kind of picture you want containing text, lines, arrows and circles. You tell LaTeX where to put things in the picture by specifying their coordinates. A coordinate is a number that may have a decimal point and a minus sign—a number like `5`, `0.3` or `-3.1416`. A coordinate specifies a length in multiples of the unit length `\unitlength`, so if `\unitlength` has been set to `1cm`, then the coordinate `2.54` specifies a length of 2.54 centimeters.

You should only change the value of `\unitlength`, using the `\setlength` command, outside of a `picture` environment. The default value is `1pt`.

A position is a pair of coordinates, such as `(2.4,-5)`, specifying the point with x-coordinate `2.4` and y-coordinate `-5`. Coordinates are specified in the usual way with respect to an origin, which is normally at the lower-left corner of the picture. Note that when a position appears as an argument, it is not enclosed in braces; the parentheses serve to delimit the argument.

The `picture` environment has one mandatory argument, which is a `position`. It specifies the size of the picture. The environment produces a rectangular box with width and height determined by this argument's x- and y-coordinates.

The `picture` environment also has an optional `position` argument, following the `size` argument, that can change the origin. (Unlike ordinary optional arguments, this argument is not contained in square brackets.) The optional argument gives the coordinates of the point at the lower-left corner of the picture (thereby determining the origin). For example, if `\unitlength` has been set to `1mm`, the command

```
\begin{picture}(100,200)(10,20)
```

produces a picture of width 100 millimeters and height 200 millimeters, whose lower-left corner is the point (10,20) and whose upper-right corner is therefore the point (110,220). When you first draw a picture, you typically omit the optional argument, leaving the origin at the lower-left corner. If you then want to modify your picture by shifting everything, you can just add the appropriate optional argument.

The environment's mandatory argument determines the nominal size of the picture. This need bear no relation to how large the picture really is; LaTeX will happily allow you to put things outside the picture, or even off the page. The picture's nominal size is used by LaTeX in determining how much room to leave for it.

Everything that appears in a picture is drawn by the `\put` command. The command

```
\put (11.3,-.3){...}
```

puts the object specified by `...` in the picture, with its reference point at coordinates $(11.3, -.3)$. The reference points for various objects will be described below.

The `\put` command creates an *LR box*. You can put anything that can go in an `\mbox` (see Section 20.1 [\mbox], page 70) in the text argument of the `\put` command. When you do this, the reference point will be the lower left corner of the box.

The `picture` commands are described in the following sections.

8.19.1 \circle

Synopsis:

```
\circle[*]{diameter}
```

The `\circle` command produces a circle with a diameter as close to the specified one as possible. The *-form of the command draws a solid circle.

Circles up to 40 pt can be drawn.

8.19.2 \makebox

Synopsis:

```
\makebox(width,height)[position]{text}
```

The `\makebox` command for the picture environment is similar to the normal `\makebox` command except that you must specify a *width* and *height* in multiples of `\unitlength`.

The optional argument, `[position]`, specifies the quadrant that your *text* appears in. You may select up to two of the following:

t   Moves the item to the top of the rectangle.

b   Moves the item to the bottom.

l   Moves the item to the left.

r   Moves the item to the right.

See Section 20.4 [\makebox], page 70.

8.19.3 \framebox

Synopsis:

> \framebox(*width*,*height*)[*pos*]{...}

The \framebox command is like \makebox (see previous section), except that it puts a frame around the outside of the box that it creates.

The \framebox command produces a rule of thickness \fboxrule, and leaves a space \fboxsep between the rule and the contents of the box.

8.19.4 \dashbox

Draws a box with a dashed line. Synopsis:

> \dashbox{*dlen*}(*rwidth*,*rheight*)[*pos*]{*text*}

\dashbox creates a dashed rectangle around *text* in a **picture** environment. Dashes are *dlen* units long, and the rectangle has overall width *rwidth* and height *rheight*. The *text* is positioned at optional *pos*.

A dashed box looks best when the *rwidth* and *rheight* are multiples of the *dlen*.

8.19.5 \frame

Synopsis:

> \frame{*text*}

The \frame command puts a rectangular frame around *text*. The reference point is the bottom left corner of the frame. No extra space is put between the frame and the object.

8.19.6 \line

Synopsis:

> \line(*xslope*,*yslope*){*length*}

The \line command draws a line with the given *length* and slope *xslope*/*yslope*.

Standard LATEX can only draw lines with $slope = x/y$, where x and y have integer values from -6 through 6. For lines of any slope, and plenty of other shapes, see pict2e and many other packages on CTAN.

8.19.7 \linethickness

The \linethickness{*dim*} command declares the thickness of horizontal and vertical lines in a picture environment to be *dim*, which must be a positive length.

\linethickness does not affect the thickness of slanted lines, circles, or the quarter circles drawn by \oval.

8.19.8 \thicklines

The \thicklines command is an alternate line thickness for horizontal and vertical lines in a picture environment; cf. Section 8.19.7 [\linethickness], page 28 and Section 8.19.9 [\thinlines], page 29.

8.19.9 \thinlines

The \thinlines command is the default line thickness for horizontal and vertical lines in a picture environment; cf. Section 8.19.7 [\linethickness], page 28 and Section 8.19.8 [\thicklines], page 29.

8.19.10 \multiput

Synopsis:

    \multiput(x,y)(delta_x,delta_y){n}{obj}

The \multiput command copies the object *obj* in a regular pattern across a picture. *obj* is first placed at position (x, y), then at $(x + \delta x, y + \delta y)$, and so on, n times.

8.19.11 \oval

Synopsis:

    \oval(width,height)[portion]

The \oval command produces a rectangle with rounded corners. The optional argument *portion* allows you to select part of the oval via the following:

t   selects the top portion;

b   selects the bottom portion;

r   selects the right portion;

l   selects the left portion.

The "corners" of the oval are made with quarter circles with a maximum radius of 20 pt, so large "ovals" will look more like boxes with rounded corners.

8.19.12 \put

Synopsis:

    \put(xcoord,ycoord){ ... }

The \put command places the material specified by the (mandatory) argument in braces at the given coordinate, (*xcoord,ycoord*).

8.19.13 \shortstack

Synopsis:

    \shortstack[position]{...\\...\\...}

The \shortstack command produces a stack of objects. The valid positions are:

r   Move the objects to the right of the stack.

l   Move the objects to the left of the stack

c   Move the objects to the centre of the stack (default)

Objects are separated with \\.

8.19.14 \vector

Synopsis:

> \vector(*xslope*,*yslope*){*length*}

The \vector command draws a line with an arrow of the specified length and slope. The *xslope* and *yslope* values must lie between −4 and +4, inclusive.

8.20 quotation

Synopsis:

> \begin{quotation}
> *text*
> \end{quotation}

The margins of the quotation environment are indented on both the left and the right. The text is justified at both margins. Leaving a blank line between text produces a new paragraph.

Unlike the quote environment, each paragraph is indented normally.

8.21 quote

Synopsis:

> \begin{quote}
> *text*
> \end{quote}

The margins of the quote environment are indented on both the left and the right. The text is justified at both margins. Leaving a blank line between text produces a new paragraph.

Unlike the quotation environment, paragraphs are not indented.

8.22 tabbing

Synopsis:

> \begin{tabbing}
> *row1col1* \= *row1col2* \= *row1col3* \= *row1col4* \\
> *row2col1* \>   \> *row2col3* \\
> ...
> \end{tabbing}

The tabbing environment provides a way to align text in columns. It works by setting tab stops and tabbing to them much as was done on an ordinary typewriter. It is best suited for cases where the width of each column is constant and known in advance.

This environment can be broken across pages, unlike the tabular environment.

The following commands can be used inside a tabbing environment:

\\ (tabbing)

> End a line.

\= (tabbing)

> Sets a tab stop at the current position.

\> (tabbing)

> Advances to the next tab stop.

\<   Put following text to the left of the local margin (without changing the margin). Can only be used at the start of the line.

\+   Moves the left margin of the next and all the following commands one tab stop to the right, beginning tabbed line if necessary.

\-   Moves the left margin of the next and all the following commands one tab stop to the left, beginning tabbed line if necessary.

\' (tabbing)

> Moves everything that you have typed so far in the current column, i.e. everything from the most recent \>, \<, \', \\, or \kill command, to the right of the previous column, flush against the current column's tab stop.

\' (tabbing)

> Allows you to put text flush right against any tab stop, including tab stop 0. However, it can't move text to the right of the last column because there's no tab stop there. The \' command moves all the text that follows it, up to the \\ or \end{tabbing} command that ends the line, to the right margin of the tabbing environment. There must be no \> or \' command between the \' and the command that ends the line.

\a (tabbing)

> In a tabbing environment, the commands \=, \' and \' do not produce accents as usual (see Section 21.3 [Accents], page 76). Instead, the commands \a=, \a' and \a' are used.

\kill   Sets tab stops without producing text. Works just like \\ except that it throws away the current line instead of producing output for it. The effect of any \=, \+ or \- commands in that line remain in effect.

\poptabs   Restores the tab stop positions saved by the last \pushtabs.

\pushtabs

> Saves all current tab stop positions. Useful for temporarily changing tab stop positions in the middle of a tabbing environment.

\tabbingsep

> Distance to left of tab stop moved by \'.

This example typesets a Pascal function in a traditional format:

```
\begin{tabbing}
function \= fact(n : integer) : integer;\\
        \> begin \= \+ \\
              \> if \= n $>$ 1 then \+ \\
                     fact := n * fact(n-1) \- \\
                 else \+ \\
                     fact := 1; \-\- \\
              end;\\
\end{tabbing}
```

8.23 `table`

Synopsis:

```
\begin{table}[placement]

 body of the table

\caption{table title}
\end{table}
```

Tables are objects that are not part of the normal text, and are usually "floated" to a convenient place, like the top of a page. Tables will not be split between two pages.

The optional argument *placement* determines where LATEX will try to place your table. There are four places where LATEX can possibly put a float; these are the same as that used with the `figure` environment, and described there (see Section 8.10 [figure], page 20).

The standard `report` and `article` classes use the default placement `[tbp]`.

The body of the table is made up of whatever text, LATEX commands, etc., you wish. The `\caption` command allows you to title your table.

8.24 `tabular`

Synopsis:

```
\begin{tabular}[pos]{cols}
column 1 entry & column 2 entry ... & column n entry \\
...
\end{tabular}
```

or

```
\begin{tabular*}{width}[pos]{cols}
column 1 entry & column 2 entry ... & column n entry \\
...
\end{tabular*}
```

These environments produce a box consisting of a sequence of rows of items, aligned vertically in columns.

`\\` must be used to specify the end of each row of the table, except for the last, where it is optional—unless an `\hline` command (to put a rule below the table) follows.

The mandatory and optional arguments consist of:

width   Specifies the width of the `tabular*` environment. There must be rubber space between columns that can stretch to fill out the specified width.

pos   Specifies the vertical position; default is alignment on the centre of the environment.

        t   align on top row

        b   align on bottom row

cols   Specifies the column formatting. It consists of a sequence of the following specifiers, corresponding to the sequence of columns and intercolumn material.

l	A column of left-aligned items.
r	A column of right-aligned items.
c	A column of centered items.
|	A vertical line the full height and depth of the environment.
@{text}	This inserts *text* in every row. An @-expression suppresses the intercolumn space normally inserted between columns; any desired space before the adjacent item must be included in *text*.

To insert commands that are automatically executed before a given column, you have to load the **array** package and use the >{...} specifier.

An \extracolsep{wd} command in an @-expression causes an extra space of width **wd** to appear to the left of all subsequent columns, until countermanded by another \extracolsep command. Unlike ordinary intercolumn space, this extra space is not suppressed by an @-expression. An \extracolsep command can be used only in an @-expression in the **cols** argument.

p{wd}   Produces a column with each item typeset in a parbox of width *wd*, as if it were the argument of a \parbox[t]{wd} command. However, a \\ may not appear in the item, except in the following situations:

1. inside an environment like **minipage**, **array**, or **tabular**.
2. inside an explicit \parbox.
3. in the scope of a \centering, \raggedright, or \raggedleft declaration. The latter declarations must appear inside braces or an environment when used in a p-column element.

*{num}{cols}

Equivalent to *num* copies of *cols*, where *num* is a positive integer and *cols* is any list of column-specifiers, which may contain another *-expression.

Parameters that control formatting:

\arrayrulewidth

Thickness of the rule created by |, \hline, and \vline in the **tabular** and **array** environments; the default is '.4pt'.

\arraystretch

Scaling of spacing between rows in the **tabular** and **array** environments; default is '1', for no scaling.

\doublerulesep

Horizontal distance between the vertical rules produced by || in the **tabular** and **array** environments; default is '2pt'.

\tabcolsep

Half the width of the space between columns; default is '6pt'.

The following commands can be used inside a **tabular** environment:

8.24.1 \multicolumn

Synopsis:

>   \multicolumn{*cols*}{*pos*}{*text*}

The \multicolumn command makes an entry that spans several columns. The first mandatory argument, *cols*, specifies the number of columns to span. The second mandatory argument, *pos*, specifies the formatting of the entry; c for centered, l for flushleft, r for flushright. The third mandatory argument, *text*, specifies what text to put in the entry.

Here's an example showing two columns separated by an en-dash; \multicolumn is used for the heading:

```
\begin{tabular}{r@{--}l}
\multicolumn{2}{c}{\bf Unicode}\cr
    0x80&0x7FF    \cr
   0x800&0xFFFF   \cr
0x10000&0x1FFFF \cr
\end{tabular}
```

8.24.2 \cline

Synopsis:

>   \cline{*i-j*}

The \cline command draws horizontal lines across the columns specified, beginning in column *i* and ending in column *j*, which are specified in the mandatory argument.

8.24.3 \hline

The \hline command draws a horizontal line the width of the enclosing tabular or array environment. It's most commonly used to draw a line at the top, bottom, and between the rows of a table.

8.24.4 \vline

The \vline command will draw a vertical line extending the full height and depth of its row. An \hfill command can be used to move the line to the edge of the column. It can also be used in an @-expression.

8.25 thebibliography

Synopsis:

>   \begin{thebibliography}{*widest-label*}
>   \bibitem[*label*]{*cite_key*}
>
>   ...
>
>   \end{thebibliography}

The thebibliography environment produces a bibliography or reference list.

In the article class, this reference list is labelled "References"; in the report class, it is labelled "Bibliography". You can change the label (in the standard classes) by redefining the command \refname. For instance, this eliminates it entirely:

```
\renewcommand{\refname}{}
```

The mandatory *widest-label* argument is text that, when typeset, is as wide as the widest item label produced by the \bibitem commands. It is typically given as 9 for bibliographies with less than 10 references, 99 for ones with less than 100, etc.

8.25.1 \bibitem

Synopsis:

```
\bibitem[label]{cite_key}
```

The \bibitem command generates an entry labelled by *label*. If the *label* argument is missing, a number is automatically generated using the **enumi** counter. The *cite_key* is any sequence of letters, numbers, and punctuation symbols not containing a comma.

This command writes an entry to the .aux file containing the item's *cite_key* and label. When the .aux file is read by the \begin{document} command, the item's label is associated with **cite_key**, causing references to *cite_key* with a \cite command (see next section) to produce the associated label.

8.25.2 \cite

Synopsis:

```
\cite[subcite]{keys}
```

The *keys* argument is a list of one or more citation keys, separated by commas. This command generates an in-text citation to the references associated with *keys* by entries in the .aux file.

The text of the optional *subcite* argument appears after the citation. For example, \cite[p.~314]{knuth} might produce '[Knuth, p. 314]'.

8.25.3 \nocite

\nocite{keys}

The \nocite command produces no text, but writes *keys*, which is a list of one or more citation keys, to the .aux file.

8.25.4 Using BibTEX

If you use the BibTEX program by Oren Patashnik (highly recommended if you need a bibliography of more than a couple of titles) to maintain your bibliography, you don't use the **thebibliography** environment (see Section 8.25 [thebibliography], page 34). Instead, you include the lines

```
\bibliographystyle{bibstyle}
\bibliography{bibfile1,bibfile2}
```

The \bibliographystyle command does not produce any output of its own. Rather, it defines the style in which the bibliography will be produced: *bibstyle* refers to a file *bibstyle*.bst, which defines how your citations will look. The standard *style* names distributed with BibTEX are:

alpha   Sorted alphabetically. Labels are formed from name of author and year of publication.

plain   Sorted alphabetically. Labels are numeric.

unsrt   Like plain, but entries are in order of citation.

abbrv   Like plain, but more compact labels.

In addition, numerous other BibTEX style files exist tailored to the demands of various publications. See `http://mirror.ctan.org/biblio/bibtex/contrib`.

The \bibliography command is what actually produces the bibliography. The argument to \bibliography refers to files named *bibfile*.bib, which should contain your database in BibTEX format. Only the entries referred to via \cite and \nocite will be listed in the bibliography.

8.26 theorem

Synopsis:

```
\begin{theorem}
theorem-text
\end{theorem}
```

The theorem environment produces "Theorem *n*" in boldface followed by *theorem-text*, where the numbering possibilities for *n* are described under \newtheorem (see Section 12.6 [\newtheorem], page 44).

8.27 titlepage

Synopsis:

```
\begin{titlepage}
text
\end{titlepage}
```

The titlepage environment creates a title page, i.e., a page with no printed page number or heading. It also causes the following page to be numbered page one. Formatting the title page is left to you. The \today command may be useful on title pages (see Section 21.6 [\today], page 78).

You can use the \maketitle command (see Section 18.1 [\maketitle], page 65) to produce a standard title page without a titlepage environment.

8.28 verbatim

Synopsis:

```
\begin{verbatim}
literal-text
\end{verbatim}
```

The verbatim environment is a paragraph-making environment in which LATEX produces exactly what you type in; for instance the \ character produces a printed '\'. It turns LATEX into a typewriter with carriage returns and blanks having the same effect that they would on a typewriter.

The verbatim uses a monospaced typewriter-like font (\tt).

8.28.1 \verb

Synopsis:

```
\verbcharliteral-textchar
\verb*charliteral-textchar
```

The \verb command typesets *literal-text* as it is input, including special characters and spaces, using the typewriter (\tt) font. No spaces are allowed between \verb or \verb* and the delimiter *char*, which begins and ends the verbatim text. The delimiter must not appear in *literal-text*.

The *-form differs only in that spaces are printed with a "visible space" character. (Namely, ␣.)

8.29 verse

Synopsis:

```
\begin{verse}
line1 \\
line2 \\
...
\end{verse}
```

The verse environment is designed for poetry, though you may find other uses for it.

The margins are indented on the left and the right, paragraphs are not indented, and the text is not justified. Separate the lines of each stanza with \\, and use one or more blank lines to separate the stanzas.

9 Line breaking

The first thing LaTeX does when processing ordinary text is to translate your input file into a sequence of glyphs and spaces. To produce a printed document, this sequence must be broken into lines (and these lines must be broken into pages).

LaTeX usually does the line (and page) breaking for you, but in some environments, you do the line breaking yourself with the \\ command, and you can always manually force breaks.

9.1 \\[*][*morespace*]

The \\ command tells LaTeX to start a new line. It has an optional argument, *morespace*, that specifies how much extra vertical space is to be inserted before the next line. This can be a negative amount.

The * command is the same as the ordinary \\ command except that it tells LaTeX not to start a new page after the line.

9.2 \obeycr & \restorecr

The \obeycr command makes a return in the input file ('^^M', internally) the same as \\ (followed by \relax). So each new line in the input will also be a new line in the output.

\restorecr restores normal line-breaking behavior.

9.3 \newline

The \newline command breaks the line at the present point, with no stretching of the text before it. It can only be used in paragraph mode.

9.4 \- (discretionary hyphen)

The \- command tells LaTeX that it may hyphenate the word at that point. LaTeX is pretty good at hyphenating, and usually finds most of the correct hyphenation points, while almost never using an incorrect one. The \- command is used for the exceptional cases.

When you insert \- commands in a word, the word will only be hyphenated at those points and not at any of the hyphenation points that LaTeX might otherwise have chosen.

9.5 \fussy

The declaration \fussy (which is the default) makes TeX picky about line breaking. This usually avoids too much space between words, at the cost of an occasional overfull box.

This command cancels the effect of a previous \sloppy command (see Section 9.6 [\sloppy], page 38.

9.6 \sloppy

The declaration \sloppy makes TeX less fussy about line breaking. This will avoid overfull boxes, at the cost of loose interword spacing.

Lasts until a \fussy command is issued (see Section 9.5 [\fussy], page 38).

9.7 \hyphenation

Synopsis:

    \hyphenation{*word-one word-two*}

The \hyphenation command declares allowed hyphenation points with a – character in the given words. The words are separated by spaces. TeX will only hyphenate if the word matches exactly, no inflections are tried. Multiple \hyphenation commands accumulate. Some examples (the default TeX hyphenation patterns misses the hyphenations in these words):

    \hyphenation{ap-pen-dix col-umns data-base data-bases}

9.8 \linebreak & \nolinebreak

Synopses:

    \linebreak[*priority*]
    \nolinebreak[*priority*]

By default, the \linebreak (\nolinebreak) command forces (prevents) a line break at the current position. For \linebreak, the spaces in the line are stretched out so that it extends to the right margin as usual.

With the optional argument *priority*, you can convert the command from a demand to a request. The *priority* must be a number from 0 to 4. The higher the number, the more insistent the request.

10 Page breaking

LaTeX starts new pages asynchronously, when enough material has accumulated to fill up a page. Usually this happens automatically, but sometimes you may want to influence the breaks.

10.1 \cleardoublepage

The \cleardoublepage command ends the current page and causes all figures and tables that have so far appeared in the input to be printed. In a two-sided printing style, it also makes the next page a right-hand (odd-numbered) page, producing a blank page if necessary.

10.2 \clearpage

The \clearpage command ends the current page and causes all figures and tables that have so far appeared in the input to be printed.

10.3 \newpage

The \newpage command ends the current page, but does not clear floats (see \clearpage above).

10.4 \enlargethispage

\enlargethispage{size}

   \enlargethispage*{size}

Enlarge the \textheight for the current page by the specified amount; e.g. \enlargethispage{\baselineskip} will allow one additional line.

The starred form tries to squeeze the material together on the page as much as possible. This is normally used together with an explicit \pagebreak.

10.5 \pagebreak & \nopagebreak

Synopses:

   \pagebreak[priority]
   \nopagebreak[priority]

By default, the \pagebreak (\nopagebreak) command forces (prevents) a page break at the current position. With \pagebreak, the vertical space on the page is stretched out where possible so that it extends to the normal bottom margin.

With the optional argument priority, you can convert the \pagebreak command from a demand to a request. The number must be a number from 0 to 4. The higher the number, the more insistent the request is.

11 Footnotes

Footnotes can be produced in one of two ways. They can be produced with one command, the \footnote command. They can also be produced with two commands, the \footnotemark and the \footnotetext commands.

11.1 \footnote

Synopsis:

    \footnote[number]{text}

The \footnote command places the numbered footnote *text* at the bottom of the current page. The optional argument *number* changes the default footnote number.

This command can only be used in outer paragraph mode; i.e., you cannot use it in sectioning commands like \chapter, in figures, tables or in a tabular environment. (See following sections.)

11.2 \footnotemark

With no optional argument, the \footnotemark command puts the current footnote number in the text. This command can be used in inner paragraph mode. You give the text of the footnote separately, with the \footnotetext command.

This command can be used to produce several consecutive footnote markers referring to the same footnote with

    \footnotemark[\value{footnote}]

after the first \footnote command.

11.3 \footnotetext

Synopsis:

    \footnotetext[number]{text}

The \footnotetext command places *text* at the bottom of the page as a footnote. This command can come anywhere after the \footnotemark command. The \footnotetext command must appear in outer paragraph mode.

The optional argument *number* changes the default footnote number.

11.4 Symbolic footnotes

If you want to use symbols for footnotes, rather than increasing numbers, redefine \thefootnote like this:

    \renewcommand{\thefootnote}{\fnsymbol{footnote}}

The \fnsymbol command produces a predefined series of symbols (see Section 13.1 [\alph \Alph \arabic \roman \Roman \fnsymbol], page 46). If you want to use a different symbol as your footnote mark, you'll need to also redefine \@fnsymbol.

11.5 Footnote parameters

`\footnoterule`

> Produces the rule separating the main text on a page from the page's footnotes. Default dimensions: `0.4pt` thick (or wide), and `0.4\columnwidth` long in the standard document classes (except `slides`, where it does not appear).

`\footnotesep`

> The height of the strut placed at the beginning of the footnote. By default, this is set to the normal strut for `\footnotesize` fonts (see Section 4.2 [Font sizes], page 10), therefore there is no extra space between footnotes. This is '`6.65pt`' for '`10pt`', '`7.7pt`' for '`11pt`', and '`8.4pt`' for '`12pt`'.

12 Definitions

LaTeX has support for making new commands of many different kinds.

12.1 \newcommand & \renewcommand

\newcommand and \renewcommand define and redefine a command, respectively. Synopses:

    \newcommand[*]{cmd}[nargs][optargval]{defn}
    \renewcommand[*]{cmd}[nargs][optargval]{defn}

*	The *-form of these commands requires that the arguments not contain multiple paragraphs of text (not \long, in plain TeX terms).
cmd	The command name, beginning with \. For \newcommand, it must not be already defined and must not begin with \end; for \renewcommand, it must already be defined.
nargs	An optional integer from 1 to 9 specifying the number of arguments that the command will take. The default is for the command to have no arguments.
optargval	If this optional parameter is present, it means that the first argument of command *cmd* is optional and its default value (i.e., if it is not specified in the call) is *optarg*. In otherwise, when calling the macro, if no [value] is given after *cmd*—which is different from having [] for an empty *value*—then string 'optargval' becomes the value of #1 within *defn* when the macro is expanded.
defn	The text to be substituted for every occurrence of cmd; a construct of the form #n in *defn* is replaced by the text of the *n*th argument.

12.2 \newcounter

Synopsis:

    \newcounter{countername}[supercounter]

The \newcounter command globally defines a new counter named *countername*. The new counter is initialized to zero.

If the optional argument [supercounter] appears then *countername* will be numbered within, or subsidiary to, the existing counter *supercounter*. For example, ordinarily subsection is numbered within section. Any time *supercounter* is incremented with \stepcounter (see Section 13.7 [\stepcounter], page 48) or \refstepcounter (see Section 13.6 [\refstepcounter], page 47) then *counter* is reset to zero. See Chapter 13 [Counters], page 46, for more information about counters.

Note that the name of each counter does not begin with a backslash (\).

12.3 \newlength

Synopsis:

    \newlength{\arg}

The \newlength command defines the mandatory argument as a *length* command with a value of zero. The argument must be a control sequence, as in \newlength{\foo}. An error occurs if \foo is already defined.

See Chapter 14 [Lengths], page 49, for how to set the new length to a nonzero value, and for more information about lengths in general.

12.4 \newsavebox

Synopsis:

>   \newsavebox{*cmd*}

Defines *cmd*, which must be a command name not already defined, to refer to a new bin for storing boxes.

12.5 \newenvironment & \renewenvironment

Synopses:

>   \newenvironment[*] {*env*} [*nargs*] [*default*] {*begdef*}{*enddef*}
>   \renewenvironment[*] {*env*} [*nargs*] {*begdef*}{*enddef*}

These commands define or redefine an environment *env*, that is, \begin{*env*} ... \end{*env*}.

*	The *-form of these commands requires that the arguments (not the contents of the environment) not contain multiple paragraphs of text.
env	The name of the environment. For \newenvironment, *env* must not be an existing environment, and the command *env* must be undefined. For \renewenvironment, *env* must be the name of an existing environment.
nargs	An integer from 1 to 9 denoting the number of arguments of the newly-defined environment. The default is no arguments.
default	If this is specified, the first argument is optional, and *default* gives the default value for that argument.
begdef	The text expanded at every occurrence of \begin{*env*}; a construct of the form #n in *begdef* is replaced by the text of the *n*th argument.
enddef	The text expanded at every occurrence of \end{*env*}. It may not contain any argument parameters.

12.6 \newtheorem

>   \newtheorem{*newenv*}{*label*}[*within*]
>   \newtheorem{*newenv*}[*numbered_like*]{*label*}

This command defines a theorem-like environment. Arguments:

newenv	The name of the environment to be defined; must not be the name of an existing environment or otherwise defined.
label	The text printed at the beginning of the environment, before the number. For example, 'Theorem'.
numbered_like	(Optional.) The name of an already defined theorem-like environment; the new environment will be numbered just like *numbered_like*.

within   (Optional.) The name of an already defined counter, a sectional unit. The new theorem counter will be reset at the same time as the *within* counter.

At most one of *numbered_like* and *within* can be specified, not both.

12.7 \newfont

Synopsis:

> \newfont{*cmd*}{*fontname*}

Defines a control sequence *cmd*, which must not already be defined, to make *fontname* be the current font. The file looked for on the system is named `fontname.tfm`.

This is a low-level command for setting up to use an individual font. More commonly, fonts are defined in families through `.fd` files.

12.8 \protect

Footnotes, line breaks, any command that has an optional argument, and many more are so-called *fragile* commands. When a fragile command is used in certain contexts, called *moving arguments*, it must be preceded by \protect. In addition, any fragile commands within the arguments must have their own \protect.

Some examples of moving arguments are \caption (see Section 8.10 [figure], page 20), \thanks (see Section 18.1 [\maketitle], page 65), and expressions in `tabular` and `array` environments (see Section 8.24 [tabular], page 32).

Commands which are not fragile are called *robust*. They must not be preceded by \protect.

See also:

`http://www-h.eng.cam.ac.uk/help/tpl/textprocessing/teTeX/latex/latex2e-html/fragile.html`
`http://www.tex.ac.uk/cgi-bin/texfaq2html?label=protect`

13 Counters

Everything LaTeX numbers for you has a counter associated with it. The name of the counter is often the same as the name of the environment or command associated with the number, except with no backslash (\). Thus the `\chapter` command starts a chapter and the `chapter` counter keeps track of the chapter number. Below is a list of the counters used in LaTeX's standard document classes to control numbering.

part	paragraph	figure	enumi
chapter	subparagraph	table	enumii
section	page	footnote	enumiii
subsection	equation	mpfootnote	enumiv
subsubsection			

The `mpfootnote` counter is used by the `\footnote` command inside of a minipage (see Section 8.18 [minipage], page 26).

The `enumi` through `enumiv` counters are used in the `enumerate` environment, for up to four nested levels (see Section 8.7 [enumerate], page 19).

New counters are created with `\newcounter`. See Section 12.2 [\newcounter], page 43.

13.1 \alph \Alph \arabic \roman \Roman \fnsymbol: Printing counters

All of these commands take a single counter as an argument, for instance, `\alph{enumi}`. Note that the counter name does not start with a backslash.

`\alph`   prints *counter* using lowercase letters: 'a', 'b', . . .

`\Alph`   uses uppercase letters: 'A', 'B', . . .

`\arabic`   uses Arabic numbers: '1', '2', . . .

`\roman`   uses lowercase roman numerals: 'i', 'ii', . . .

`\Roman`   uses uppercase roman numerals: 'I', 'II', . . .

`\fnsymbol`

  prints the value of *counter* in a specific sequence of nine symbols (conventionally used for labeling footnotes). The value of *counter* must be between 1 and 9, inclusive.

  Here are the symbols (as Unicode code points in ASCII output):

    asterisk(*) dagger(‡) ddagger(‡)
    section-sign(§) paragraph-sign(¶) parallel(∥)
    double-asterisk(**) double-dagger(††) double-ddagger(‡‡)

13.2 \usecounter{*counter*}

Synopsis:

    \usecounter{*counter*}

In the `list` environment, when used in the second argument, this command sets up *counter* to number the list items. It initializes *counter* to zero, and arranges that when `\item` is called without its optional argument then *counter* is incremented by \refstepcounter, making its value be the current ref value. This command is fragile (see Section 12.8 [\protect], page 45).

Put in the preamble, this makes a new list environment enumerated with *testcounter*:

```
\newcounter{testcounter}
\newenvironment{test}{%
  \begin{list}{}{%
    \usecounter{testcounter}
  }
}{%
  \end{list}
}
```

13.3 \value{*counter*}

Synopsis:

```
\value{counter}
```

The \value command produces the value of *counter*. It can be used anywhere LaTeX expects a number, for example:

```
\setcounter{myctr}{3}
\addtocounter{myctr}{1}
\hspace{\value{myctr}\parindent}
```

13.4 \setcounter{*counter*}{*value*}

Synopsis:

```
\setcounter{counter}{value}
```

The \setcounter command globally sets the value of *counter* to the *value* argument. Note that the counter name does not start with a backslash.

13.5 \addtocounter{*counter*}{*value*}

The \addtocounter command globally increments *counter* by the amount specified by the *value* argument, which may be negative.

13.6 \refstepcounter{*counter*}

The \refstepcounter command works in the same way as \stepcounter (see Section 13.7 [\stepcounter], page 48), meaning that it globally increments the value of *counter* by one and resets the value of any counter numbered within it. (For the definition of counters numbered within this one, see Section 12.2 [\newcounter], page 43.) In addition, this command also defines the current \ref value to be the result of \thecounter. Note that while setting the counter is done globally, setting the current \ref value is only valid inside the current group.

13.7 \stepcounter{*counter*}

The \stepcounter command globally adds one to *counter* and resets all counters numbered within it. (For the definition of counters numbered within this one, see Section 12.2 [\newcounter], page 43.)

13.8 \day \month \year: **Predefined counters**

LaTeX defines counters for the day of the month (\day, 1–31), month of the year (\month, 1–12), and year (\year, Common Era). When TeX starts up, they are set to the current values on the system where TeX is running. They are not updated as the job progresses.

The related command \today produces a string representing the current day (see Section 21.6 [\today], page 78).

14 Lengths

A `length` is a measure of distance. Many LaTeX commands take a length as an argument.

14.1 \setlength{\len}{value}

The \setlength sets the value of \len to the *value* argument, which can be expressed in any units that LaTeX understands, i.e., inches (`in`), millimeters (`mm`), points (`pt`), big points (`bp`, etc.

14.2 \addtolength{\len}{amount}

The \addtolength command increments a "length command" \len by the amount specified in the *amount* argument, which may be negative.

14.3 \settodepth

\settodepth{\gnat}{text}

   The \settodepth command sets the value of a `length` command equal to the depth of the `text` argument.

14.4 \settoheight

\settoheight{\gnat}{text}

   The \settoheight command sets the value of a `length` command equal to the height of the `text` argument.

14.5 \settowidth{\len}{text}

The \settowidth command sets the value of the command \len to the width of the *text* argument.

14.6 Predefined lengths

\width

   \height

   \depth

   \totalheight

   These length parameters can be used in the arguments of the box-making commands (see Chapter 20 [Boxes], page 70). They specify the natural width, etc., of the text in the box. \totalheight equals \height + \depth. To make a box with the text stretched to double the natural size, e.g., say

   \makebox[2\width]{Get a stretcher}

15 Making paragraphs

A paragraph is ended by one or more completely blank lines—lines not containing even a %. A blank line should not appear where a new paragraph cannot be started, such as in math mode or in the argument of a sectioning command.

15.1 \indent

\indent produces a horizontal space whose width equals the width of the \parindent length, the normal paragraph indentation. It is used to add paragraph indentation where it would otherwise be suppressed.

The default value for \parindent is 1em in two-column mode, otherwise 15pt for 10pt documents, 17pt for 11pt, and 1.5em for 12pt.

15.2 \noindent

When used at the beginning of the paragraph, \noindent suppresses any paragraph indentation. It has no effect when used in the middle of a paragraph.

15.3 \parskip

\parskip is a rubber length defining extra vertical space added before each paragraph. The default is 0pt plus1pt.

15.4 Marginal notes

Synopsis:

    \marginpar[left]{right}

The \marginpar command creates a note in the margin. The first line of the note will have the same baseline as the line in the text where the \marginpar occurs.

When you only specify the mandatory argument *right*, the text will be placed

- in the right margin for one-sided layout;
- in the outside margin for two-sided layout;
- in the nearest margin for two-column layout.

The command \reversemarginpar places subsequent marginal notes in the opposite (inside) margin. \normalmarginpar places them in the default position.

When you specify both arguments, *left* is used for the left margin, and *right* is used for the right margin.

The first word will normally not be hyphenated; you can enable hyphenation there by beginning the node with \hspace{0pt}.

These parameters affect the formatting of the note:

\marginparpush

> Minimum vertical space between notes; default '7pt' for '12pt' documents, '5pt' else.

\marginparsep

>   Horizontal space between the main text and the note; default '11pt' for '10pt' documents, '10pt' else.

\marginparwidth

>   Width of the note itself; default for a one-sided '10pt' document is '90pt', '83pt' for '11pt', and '68pt' for '12pt'; '17pt' more in each case for a two-sided document. In two column mode, the default is '48pt'.

The standard LaTeX routine for marginal notes does not prevent notes from falling off the bottom of the page.

16 Math formulas

There are three environments that put LaTeX in math mode:

math   For formulas that appear right in the text.

displaymath
      For formulas that appear on their own line.

equation   The same as the displaymath environment except that it adds an equation number in the right margin.

The math environment can be used in both paragraph and LR mode, but the displaymath and equation environments can be used only in paragraph mode. The math and displaymath environments are used so often that they have the following short forms:

     \(...\)   instead of   \begin{math}...\end{math}
     \[...\]   instead of   \begin{displaymath}...\end{displaymath}

In fact, the math environment is so common that it has an even shorter form:

     $ ... $ instead of   \(...\)

The \boldmath command changes math letters and symbols to be in a bold font. It is used *outside* of math mode. Conversely, the \unboldmath command changes math glyphs to be in a normal font; it too is used *outside* of math mode.

The \displaystyle declaration forces the size and style of the formula to be that of displaymath, e.g., with limits above and below summations. For example

     $\displaystyle \sum_{n=0}^\infty x_n $

16.1 Subscripts & superscripts

To get an expression *exp* to appear as a subscript, you just type _{*exp*}. To get *exp* to appear as a superscript, you type ^{*exp*}. LaTeX handles superscripted superscripts and all of that stuff in the natural way. It even does the right thing when something has both a subscript and a superscript.

16.2 Math symbols

LaTeX provides almost any mathematical symbol you're likely to need. The commands for generating them can be used only in math mode. For example, if you include π in your source, you will get the pi symbol (π) in your output.

\|

\aleph $\aleph$

\alpha α

\amalg $\amalg$ (binary operation)

\angle $\angle$

\approx $\approx$ (relation)

\ast $*$ (binary operation)

`\asymp`   ≍ (relation)

`\backslash`
             \ (delimiter)

`\beta` β

`\bigcap`   ∩

`\bigcirc`   ◯ (binary operation)

`\bigcup`   ∪

`\bigodot`   ⊙

`\bigoplus`
             ⊕

`\bigotimes`
             ⊗

`\bigtriangledown`
             ▽ (binary operation)

`\bigtriangleup`
             △ (binary operation)

`\bigsqcup`
             ⊔

`\biguplus`
             ⊎

`\bigvee`   ⋁

`\bigwedge`
             ⋀

`\bot`   ⊥

`\bowtie`   ⋈ (relation)

`\Box`   (square open box symbol)

`\bullet`   • (binary operation)

`\cap`   ∩ (binary operation)

`\cdot`   · (binary operation)

`\chi` χ

`\circ`   ∘ (binary operation)

`\clubsuit`
             ♣

`\cong`   ≅ (relation)

`\coprod`   ∐

\cup	∪ (binary operation)
\dagger	† (binary operation)
\dashv	⊣ (relation)
\ddagger	‡ (binary operation)
\Delta	Δ
\delta	δ
\Diamond	bigger ◇
\diamond	◇ (binary operation)
\diamondsuit	◇
\div	÷ (binary operation)
\doteq	≐ (relation)
\downarrow	↓ (delimiter)
\Downarrow	⇓ (delimiter)
\ell	ℓ
\emptyset	∅
\epsilon	ε
\equiv	≡ (relation)
\eta	η
\exists	∃
\flat	♭
\forall	∀
\frown	⌢ (relation)
\Gamma	Γ
\gamma	γ
\ge	≥
\geq	≥ (relation)
\gets	←
\gg	≫ (relation)
\hbar	ℏ
\heartsuit	♡

`\hookleftarrow`
$\hookleftarrow$

`\hookrightarrow`
$\hookrightarrow$

`\iff` $\iff$

`\Im` $\Im$

`\in` $\in$ (relation)

`\infty` ∞

`\int` $\int$

`\iota` ι

`\Join`   condensed bowtie symbol (relation)

`\kappa` κ

`\Lambda` Λ

`\lambda` λ

`\land` $\land$

`\langle` $\langle$ (delimiter)

`\lbrace` $\lbrace$ (delimiter)

`\lbrack` $\lbrack$ (delimiter)

`\lceil` $\lceil$ (delimiter)

`\le` $\le$

`\leadsto`

`\Leftarrow`
$\Leftarrow$

`\leftarrow`
$\leftarrow$

`\leftharpoondown`
$\leftharpoondown$

`\leftharpoonup`
$\leftharpoonup$

`\Leftrightarrow`
$\Leftrightarrow$

`\leftrightarrow`
$\leftrightarrow$

`\leq` $\leq$ (relation)

`\lfloor` $\lfloor$ (delimiter)

\lhd	(left-pointing arrow head)
\ll	≪ (relation)
\lnot	¬
\longleftarrow	
	⟵
\longleftrightarrow	
	⟷
\longmapsto	
	⟼
\longrightarrow	
	⟶
\lor	∨
\mapsto	↦
\mho	(glyph not available; it is an upside down Omega)
\mid		(relation)
\models	⊨ (relation)
\mp	∓ (binary operation)
\mu	μ
\nabla	∇
\natural	♮
\ne	≠
\nearrow	↗
\neg	¬
\neq	≠ (relation)
\ni	∋ (relation)
\not	Overstrike a following operator with a /, as in ≠.
\notin	∉
\nu	ν
\nwarrow	↖
\odot	⊙ (binary operation)
\oint	∮
\Omega	Ω
\omega	ω
\ominus	⊖ (binary operation)

\oplus	$\oplus$	(binary operation)
\oslash	$\oslash$	(binary operation)
\otimes	$\otimes$	(binary operation)
\owns	$\ni$	
\parallel		
	$\parallel$	(relation)
\partial	∂	
\perp	$\perp$	(relation)
\phi	ϕ	
\Pi	Π	
\pi	π	
\pm	$\pm$	(binary operation)
\prec	$\prec$	(relation)
\preceq	$\preceq$	(relation)
\prime	$\prime$	
\prod	$\prod$	
\propto	$\propto$	(relation)
\Psi	Ψ	
\psi	ψ	
\rangle	$\rangle$	(delimiter)
\rbrace	$\}$	(delimiter)
\rbrack	$]$	(delimiter)
\rceil	$\rceil$	(delimiter)
\Re	$\Re$	
\rfloor	$\rfloor$	
\rhd		(binary operation)
\rho	ρ	
\Rightarrow		
	$\Rightarrow$	
\rightarrow		
	$\rightarrow$	
\rightharpoondown		
	$\rightharpoondown$	
\rightharpoonup		
	$\rightharpoonup$	

\rightleftharpoons
            $\rightleftharpoons$

\searrow $\searrow$

\setminus
            $\setminus$ (binary operation)

\sharp $\sharp$

\Sigma Σ

\sigma σ

\sim $\sim$ (relation)

\simeq $\simeq$ (relation)

\smallint
            $\smallint$

\smile $\smile$ (relation)

\spadesuit
            $\spadesuit$

\sqcap $\sqcap$ (binary operation)

\sqcup $\sqcup$ (binary operation)

\sqsubset
            (relation)

\sqsubseteq
            $\sqsubseteq$ (relation)

\sqsupset
            (relation)

\sqsupseteq
            $\sqsupseteq$ (relation)

\star $\star$ (binary operation)

\subset $\subset$ (relation)

\subseteq
            $\subseteq$ (relation)

\succ $\succ$ (relation)

\succeq $\succeq$ (relation)

\sum $\sum$

\supset $\supset$ (relation)

\supseteq
            $\supseteq$ (relation)

\surd $\surd$

```
\swarrow    ↙

\tau        τ

\theta      θ

\times      × (binary operation)

\to         →

\top        ⊤

\triangle
            △

\triangleleft
            ◁ (binary operation)

\triangleright
            ▷ (binary operation)

\unlhd      left-pointing arrowhead with line under (binary operation)

\unrhd      right-pointing arrowhead with line under (binary operation)

\Uparrow    ⇑ (delimiter)

\uparrow    ↑ (delimiter)

\Updownarrow
            ⇕ (delimiter)

\updownarrow
            ↕ (delimiter)

\uplus      ⊎ (binary operation)

\Upsilon    ϒ

\upsilon    υ

\varepsilon
            ε

\varphi     φ

\varpi      ϖ

\varrho     ϱ

\varsigma
            ς

\vartheta
            ϑ

\vdash      ⊢ (relation)

\vee        ∨ (binary operation)

\Vert       ‖ (delimiter)
```

`\vert`	| (delimiter)
`\wedge`	∧ (binary operation)
`\wp`	℘
`\wr`	≀ (binary operation)
`\Xi`	Ξ
`\xi`	ξ
`\zeta`	ζ

16.3 Math functions

These commands produce roman function names in math mode with proper spacing.

`\arccos`	arccos
`\arcsin`	arcsin
`\arctan`	arctan
`\arg`	arg
`\bmod`	Binary modulo operator ($x \bmod y$)
`\cos`	cos
`\cosh`	cosh
`\cot`	cot
`\coth`	coth
`\csc`	csc
`\deg`	deg
`\det`	det
`\dim`	dim
`\exp`	exp
`\gcd`	gcd
`\hom`	hom
`\inf`	inf
`\ker`	ker
`\lg`	lg
`\lim`	lim
`\liminf`	lim inf
`\limsup`	lim sup
`\ln`	ln

`\log`	log
`\max`	max
`\min`	min
`\pmod`	parenthesized modulus, as in $(\quad (\bmod\ 2)^n - 1)$
`\Pr`	Pr
`\sec`	sec
`\sin`	sin
`\sinh`	sinh
`\sup`	sup
`\tan`	tan
`\tanh`	tanh

16.4 Math accents

LaTeX provides a variety of commands for producing accented letters in math. These are different from accents in normal text (see Section 21.3 [Accents], page 76).

`\acute`	Math acute accent: $\acute{x}$.
`\bar`	Math bar-over accent: $\bar{x}$.
`\breve`	Math breve accent: $\breve{x}$.
`\check`	Math háček (check) accent: $\check{x}$.
`\ddot`	Math dieresis accent: $\ddot{x}$.
`\dot`	Math dot accent: $\dot{x}$.
`\grave`	Math grave accent: $\grave{x}$.
`\hat`	Math hat (circumflex) accent: $\hat{x}$.
`\imath`	Math dotless i.
`\jmath`	Math dotless j.
`\mathring`	
	Math ring accent: $\mathring{x}$.
`\tilde`	Math tilde accent: $\tilde{x}$.
`\vec`	Math vector symbol: $\vec{x}$.
`\widehat`	Math wide hat accent: $\widehat{x+y}$.
`\widetilde`	
	Math wide tilde accent: $\widetilde{x+y}$.

16.5 Spacing in math mode

In a `math` environment, LaTeX ignores the spaces you type and puts in the spacing according to the normal rules for mathematics texts. If you want different spacing, LaTeX provides the following commands for use in math mode:

`\;`   A thick space ($\frac{5}{18}$ quad).

`\:`
`\>`   Both of these produce a medium space ($\frac{2}{9}$ quad).

`\,`   A thin space ($\frac{1}{6}$ quad); not restricted to math mode.

`\!`   A negative thin space ($-\frac{1}{6}$ quad).

16.6 Math miscellany

`\*`   A "discretionary" multiplication symbol, at which a line break is allowed.

`\cdots`   A horizontal ellipsis with the dots raised to the center of the line. As in: '$\cdots$'.

`\ddots`   A diagonal ellipsis: $\ddots$.

`\frac{num}{den}`
              Produces the fraction `num` divided by `den`.

              eg. $\frac{1}{4}$

`\left deliml ... \right delim2`
              The two delimiters need not match; '.' acts as a null delimiter, producing no output. The delimiters are sized according to the math in between. Example: `\left( \sum_i=1^10 a_i \right]`.

`\overbrace{text}`
              Generates a brace over *text*. For example, $\overbrace{x + \cdots + x}^{k \text{ times}}$.

`\overline{text}`
              Generates a horizontal line over *tex*. For example, $\overline{x + y}$.

`\sqrt[root]{arg}`
              Produces the representation of the square root of *arg*. The optional argument *root* determines what root to produce. For example, the cube root of `x+y` would be typed as `$\sqrt[3]{x+y}$`. In TeX, the result looks like this: $\sqrt[3]{x} + y$.

`\stackrel{text}{relation}`
              Puts *text* above *relation*. For example, `\stackrel{f}{\longrightarrow}`. In TeX, the result looks like this: $\stackrel{f}{\longrightarrow}$.

`\underbrace{math}`
              Generates *math* with a brace underneath. In TeX, the result looks like this: $\underbrace{x + y + z}_{>0}$.

\underline{text}
>   Causes *text*, which may be either math mode or not, to be underlined. The line is always below the text, taking account of descenders. In TEX, the result looks like this: $\underline{xyz}$

\vdots   Produces a vertical ellipsis. In TEX, the result looks like this: $\vdots$

17 Modes

When LATEX is processing your input text, it is always in one of three modes:

- Paragraph mode
- Math mode
- Left-to-right mode, called LR mode for short

Mode changes occur only when entering or leaving an environment, or when LATEX is processing the argument of certain text-producing commands.

Paragraph mode is the most common; it's the one LATEX is in when processing ordinary text. In this mode, LATEX breaks the input text into lines and breaks the lines into pages.

LATEX is in *math mode* when it's generating a mathematical formula, either displayed math or within a line.

In *LR mode*, as in paragraph mode, LATEX considers the output that it produces to be a string of words with spaces between them. However, unlike paragraph mode, LATEX keeps going from left to right; it never starts a new line in LR mode. Even if you put a hundred words into an \mbox, LATEX would keep typesetting them from left to right inside a single box (and then most likely complain because the resulting box was too wide to fit on the line). LATEX is in LR mode when it starts making a box with an \mbox command. You can get it to enter a different mode inside the box—for example, you can make it enter math mode to put a formula in the box.

There are also several text-producing commands and environments for making a box that put LATEX into paragraph mode. The box made by one of these commands or environments will be called a parbox. When LATEX is in paragraph mode while making a box, it is said to be in "inner paragraph mode" (no page breaks). Its normal paragraph mode, which it starts out in, is called "outer paragraph mode".

18 Page styles

The \documentclass command determines the size and position of the page's head and foot. The page style determines what goes in them.

18.1 \maketitle

The \maketitle command generates a title on a separate title page—except in the article class, where the title is placed at the top of the first page. Information used to produce the title is obtained from the following declarations:

\author{*name* \and *name2*}

> The \author command declares the document author(s), where the argument is a list of authors separated by \and commands. Use \\ to separate lines within a single author's entry—for example, to give the author's institution or address.

\date{*text*}

> The \date command declares *text* to be the document's date. With no \date command, the current date (see Section 21.6 [\today], page 78) is used.

\thanks{*text*}

> The \thanks command produces a \footnote to the title, usually used for credit acknowledgements.

\title{*text*}

> The \title command declares *text* to be the title of the document. Use \\ to force a line break, as usual.

18.2 \pagenumbering

Synopsis:

> \pagenumbering{*style*}

Specifies the style of page numbers, according to *style*; also resets the page number to 1. The *style* argument is one of the following:

arabic   arabic numerals

roman   lowercase Roman numerals

Roman   uppercase Roman numerals

alph   lowercase letters

Alph   uppercase letters

18.3 \pagestyle

Synopsis:

> \pagestyle{*style*}

The \pagestyle command specifies how the headers and footers are typeset from the current page onwards. Values for *style*:

plain   Just a plain page number.

empty   Empty headers and footers, e.g., no page numbers.

headings   Put running headers on each page. The document style specifies what goes in
               the headers.

myheadings
               Custom headers, specified via the \markboth or the \markright commands.

   Here are the descriptions of \markboth and \markright:

\markboth{*left*}{*right*}
               Sets both the left and the right heading. A "left-hand heading" (*left*) is gener-
               ated by the last \markboth command before the end of the page, while a "right-
               hand heading" (*right*) is generated by the first \markboth or \markright that
               comes on the page if there is one, otherwise by the last one before the page.

\markright{*right*}
               Sets the right heading, leaving the left heading unchanged.

18.4 \thispagestyle{*style*}

The \thispagestyle command works in the same manner as the \pagestyle command
(see previous section) except that it changes to *style* for the current page only.

19 Spaces

LaTeX has many ways to produce white (or filled) space.

Another space-producing command is \, to produce a "thin" space (usually 1/6 quad). It can be used in text mode, but is more often useful in math mode (see Section 16.5 [Spacing in math mode], page 62).

19.1 \hspace

Synopsis:

    \hspace[*]{length}

The \hspace command adds horizontal space. The *length* argument can be expressed in any terms that LaTeX understands: points, inches, etc. It is a rubber length. You can add both negative and positive space with an \hspace command; adding negative space is like backspacing.

LaTeX normally removes horizontal space that comes at the beginning or end of a line. To preserve this space, use the optional * form.

19.2 \hfill

The \hfill fill command produces a "rubber length" which has no natural space but can stretch or shrink horizontally as far as needed.

The \fill parameter is the rubber length itself (technically, the glue value '0pt plus1fill'); thus, \hspace\fill is equivalent to \hfill.

19.3 \SPACE: Normal interword space

The \ (space) command produces a normal interword space. It's useful after punctuation which shouldn't end a sentence. For example, `the article in Proc.\ Amer.\ Math\. Soc.\ is fundamental`. It is also often used after control sequences, as in `\TeX\ is a nice system`.

In normal circumstances, \tab and \newline are equivalent to \ .

19.4 \@: Force sentence-ending punctuation

The \@ command makes the following punctuation character end a sentence even if it normally would not. This is typically used after a capital letter. Here are side-by-side examples with and without \@:

    ... in C\@. Pascal, though ...
    ... in C. Pascal, though ...

produces

    ... in C. Pascal, though ...
    ... in C. Pascal, though ...

19.5 \thinspace: Insert 1/6 em

\thinspace produces an unbreakable and unstretchable space that is 1/6 of an em. This is the proper space to use between nested quotes, as in '".

19.6 \/: Insert italic correction

The \/ command produces an *italic correction*. This is a small space defined by the font designer for a given character, to avoid the character colliding with whatever follows. The italic *f* character typically has a large italic correction value.

If the following character is a period or comma, it's not necessary to insert an italic correction, since those punctuation symbols have a very small height. However, with semicolons or colons, as well as normal letters, it can help. Compare *f: f;* with *f: f;*.

When changing fonts with commands such as \textit{italic text} or {\itshape italic text}, LaTeX will automatically insert an italic correction if appropriate (see Section 4.1 [Font styles], page 8).

Despite the name, roman characters can also have an italic correction. Compare pdfTeX with pdfTeX.

There is no concept of italic correction in math mode; spacing is done in a different way.

19.7 \hrulefill

The \hrulefill fill command produces a "rubber length" which can stretch or shrink horizontally. It will be filled with a horizontal rule.

19.8 \dotfill

The \dotfill command produces a "rubber length" that fills with dots instead of just white space.

19.9 \addvspace

\addvspace{length}

The \addvspace command normally adds a vertical space of height length. However, if vertical space has already been added to the same point in the output by a previous \addvspace command, then this command will not add more space than is needed to make the natural length of the total vertical space equal to length.

19.10 \bigskip \medskip \smallskip

These commands produce a given amount of space, specified by the document class.

\bigskip The same as \vspace{\bigskipamount}, ordinarily about one line space, with stretch and shrink (the default for the book and article classes is 12pt plus 4pt minus 4pt).

\medskip The same as \vspace{\medskipamount}, ordinarily about half of a line space, with stretch and shrink (the default for the book and article classes is 6pt plus 2pt minus 2pt).

\smallskip

The same as \vspace{\smallskipamount}, ordinarily about a quarter of a line space, with stretch and shrink (the default for the book and article classes is 3pt plus 1pt minus 1pt).

19.11 \vfill

The \vfill fill command produces a rubber length (glue) which can stretch or shrink vertically as far as needed. It's equivalent to \vspace{\fill} (see Section 19.2 [\hfill], page 67).

19.12 \vspace[*]{length}

Synopsis:

> \vspace[*]{length}

The \vspace command adds the vertical space length, i.e., a rubber length. length can be negative or positive.

Ordinarily, LaTeX removes vertical space added by \vspace at the top or bottom of a page. With the optional * argument, the space is not removed.

20 Boxes

All the predefined length parameters (see Section 14.6 [Predefined lengths], page 49) can be used in the arguments of the box-making commands.

20.1 \mbox{*text*}

The \mbox command creates a box just wide enough to hold the text created by its argument. The *text* is not broken into lines, so it can be used to prevent hyphenation.

20.2 \fbox and \framebox

Synopses:

```
\fbox{text}
\framebox[width][position]{text}
```

The \fbox and \framebox commands are like \mbox, except that they put a frame around the outside of the box being created.

In addition, the \framebox command allows for explicit specification of the box width with the optional *width* argument (a dimension), and positioning with the optional *position* argument.

Both commands produce a rule of thickness \fboxrule (default '.4pt'), and leave a space of \fboxsep (default '3pt') between the rule and the contents of the box.

See Section 8.19.3 [\framebox (picture)], page 28, for the \framebox command in the picture environment.

20.3 lrbox

```
\begin{lrbox}{cmd} text \end{lrbox}
```

This is the environment form of \sbox.

The text inside the environment is saved in the box cmd, which must have been declared with \newsavebox.

20.4 \makebox

Synopsis:

```
\makebox[width][position]{text}
```

The \makebox command creates a box just wide enough to contain the *text* specified. The width of the box is specified by the optional *width* argument. The position of the text within the box is determined by the optional *position* argument, which may take the following values:

c   Centered (default).

l   Flush left.

r   Flush right.

s   Stretch (justify) across entire *width*; *text* must contain stretchable space for this to work.

\makebox is also used within the picture environment see Section 8.19.2 [\makebox (picture)], page 27.

20.5 \parbox

Synopsis:

> \parbox[*position*][*height*][*inner-pos*]{*width*}{*text*}

The \parbox command produces a box whose contents are created in **paragraph** mode. It should be used to make a box small pieces of text, with nothing fancy inside. In particular, you shouldn't use any paragraph-making environments inside a \parbox argument. For larger pieces of text, including ones containing a paragraph-making environment, you should use a minipage environment (see Section 8.18 [minipage], page 26).

\parbox has two mandatory arguments:

width   the width of the parbox;

text   the text that goes inside the parbox.

The optional *position* argument allows you to align either the top or bottom line in the parbox with the baseline of the surrounding text (default is top).

The optional *height* argument overrides the natural height of the box.

The *inner-pos* argument controls the placement of the text inside the box, as follows; if it is not specified, *position* is used.

t   text is placed at the top of the box.

c   text is centered in the box.

b   text is placed at the bottom of the box.

s   stretch vertically; the text must contain vertically stretchable space for this to work.

20.6 \raisebox

Synopsis:

> \raisebox{distance}[*height*][*depth*]{text}

The \raisebox command raises or lowers *text*. The first mandatory argument specifies how high *text* is to be raised (or lowered if it is a negative amount). *text* itself is processed in LR mode.

The optional arguments *height* and *depth* are dimensions. If they are specified, LaTeX treats *text* as extending a certain distance above the baseline (height) or below (depth), ignoring its natural height and depth.

20.7 \savebox

Synopsis:

> \savebox{*boxcmd*}[*width*][*pos*]{text}

This command typeset *text* in a box just as with \makebox (see Section 20.4 [\makebox], page 70), except that instead of printing the resulting box, it saves it in the box labeled

\boxcmd, which must have been declared with \newsavebox (see Section 12.4 [\newsave-box], page 44).

20.8 \sbox{\boxcmd}{text}

Synopsis:

>   \sbox{\boxcmd}{text}

\sbox types *text* in a box just as with \mbox (see Section 20.1 [\mbox], page 70) except that instead of the resulting box being included in the normal output, it is saved in the box labeled \boxcmd. \boxcmd must have been previously declared with \newsavebox (see Section 12.4 [\newsavebox], page 44).

20.9 \usebox{\boxcmd}

Synopsis:

>   \usebox{\boxcmd}

\usebox produces the box most recently saved in the bin \boxcmd by a \savebox command (see Section 20.7 [\savebox], page 71).

21 Special insertions

LATEX provides commands for inserting characters that have a special meaning do not correspond to simple characters you can type.

21.1 Reserved characters

The following characters play a special role in LATEX and are called "reserved characters" or "special characters".

> \# \$ % & ~ _ ^ \ { }

Whenever you write one of these characters into your file, LATEX will do something special. If you simply want the character to be printed as itself, include a \ in front of the character. For example, \\$ will produce \$ in your output.

One exception to this rule is \ itself, because \\ has its own special (context-dependent) meaning. A roman \ is produced by typing $\backslash$ in your file, and a typewriter \ is produced by using '\' in a verbatim command (see Section 8.28 [verbatim], page 36).

Also, \~ and \^ place tilde and circumflex accents over the following letter, as in õ and ô (see Section 21.3 [Accents], page 76); to get a standalone ~ or ^, you can again use a verbatim command.

Finally, you can access any character of the current font once you know its number by using the \symbol command. For example, the visible space character used in the \verb* command has the code decimal 32, so it can be typed as \symbol{32}.

You can also specify octal numbers with ' or hexadecimal numbers with ", so the previous example could also be written as \symbol{'40} or \symbol{"20}.

21.2 Text symbols

LATEX provides commands to generate a number of non-letter symbols in running text. Some of these, especially the more obscure ones, are not available in OT1; you may need to load the textcomp package.

\copyright
\textcopyright
          The copyright symbol, ©.

\dag   The dagger symbol (in text).

\ddag   The double dagger symbol (in text).

\LaTeX   The LATEX logo.

\LaTeXe   The LATEX2e logo.

\guillemotleft («)
\guillemotright (»)
\guilsinglleft (‹)
\guilsinglright (›)
          Double and single angle quotation marks, commonly used in French: «, », ‹, ›.

`\ldots`
`\dots`
`\textellipsis`
>   An ellipsis (three dots at the baseline): '...'. `\ldots` and `\dots` also work in math mode.

`\lq`   Left (opening) quote: '.

`\P`
`\textparagraph`
>   Paragraph sign (pilcrow).

`\pounds`
`\textsterling`
>   English pounds sterling: £.

`\quotedblbase` („)
`\quotesinglbase` (‚)
>   Double and single quotation marks on the baseline: „ and ‚.

`\rq`   Right (closing) quote: '.

`\S`   Section symbol.

`\TeX`   The TeX logo.

`\textasciicircum`
>   ASCII circumflex: ^.

`\textasciitilde`
>   ASCII tilde: ~.

`\textasteriskcentered`
>   Centered asterisk: *.

`\textbackslash`
>   Backslash: \.

`\textbar`   Vertical bar: |.

`\textbardbl`
>   Double vertical bar.

`\textbigcircle`
>   Big circle symbol.

`\textbraceleft`
>   Left brace: {.

`\textbraceright`
>   Right brace: }.

`\textbullet`
>   Bullet: •.

`\textcircled{letter}`
>   *letter* in a circle, as in ®.

`\textcompwordmark`
`\textcapitalwordmark`
`\textascenderwordmark`

>   Composite word mark (invisible). The `\textcapital...` form has the cap height of the font, while the `\textascender...` form has the ascender height.

`\textdagger`

>   Dagger: †.

`\textdaggerdbl`

>   Double dagger: ‡.

`\textdollar` (or $)

>   Dollar sign: $.

`\textemdash` (or ---)

>   Em-dash: — (for punctuation).

`\textendash` (or --)

>   En-dash: — (for ranges).

`\texteuro`

>   The Euro symbol: €.

`\textexclamdown` (or !`)

>   Upside down exclamation point: ¡.

`\textgreater`

>   Greater than: >.

`\textless`

>   Less than: <.

`\textleftarrow`

>   Left arrow.

`\textordfeminine`
`\textordmasculine`

>   Feminine and masculine ordinal symbols: ª, º.

`\textperiodcentered`

>   Centered period: ·.

`\textquestiondown` (or ?`)

>   Upside down question mark: ¿.

`\textquotedblleft` (or ``)

>   Double left quote: ".

`\textquotedblright` (or ')

>   Double right quote: ".

`\textquoteleft` (or `)

>   Single left quote: '.

`\textquoteright` (or ')

>   Single right quote: '.

`\textquotestraightbase`
`\textquotestraightdblbase`
>   Single and double straight quotes on the baseline.

`\textregistered`
>   Registered symbol: ®.

`\textrightarrow`
>   Right arrow.

`\textthreequartersemdash`
>   "Three-quarters" em-dash, between en-dash and em-dash.

`\texttrademark`
>   Trademark symbol: TM.

`\texttwelveudash`
>   "Two-thirds" em-dash, between en-dash and em-dash.

`\textunderscore`
>   Underscore: _.

`\textvisiblespace`
>   Visible space symbol.

21.3 Accents

LaTeX has wide support for many of the world's scripts and languages, through the **babel** package and related support. This section does not attempt to cover all that support. It merely lists the core LaTeX commands for creating accented characters.

The `\capital...` commands produce alternative forms for use with capital letters. These are not available with OT1.

`\"`
`\capitaldieresis`
>   Produces an umlaut (dieresis), as in ö.

`\'`
`\capitalacute`
>   Produces an acute accent, as in ó. In the **tabbing** environment, pushes current column to the right of the previous column (see Section 8.22 [tabbing], page 30).

`\.`   Produces a dot accent over the following, as in ȯ.

`\=`
`\capitalmacron`
>   Produces a macron (overbar) accent over the following, as in ō.

`\^`
`\capitalcircumflex`
>   Produces a circumflex (hat) accent over the following, as in ô.

`\``
`\capitalgrave`
>   Produces a grave accent over the following, as in ò. In the **tabbing** environment, move following text to the right margin (see Section 8.22 [tabbing], page 30).

```
\~
\capitaltilde
```
Produces a tilde accent over the following, as in ñ.

```
\b
```
Produces a bar accent under the following, as in o̱.

```
\c
\capitalcedilla
```
Produces a cedilla accent under the following, as in ç.

```
\d
\capitaldotaccent
```
Produces a dot accent under the following, as in ọ.

```
\H
\capitalhungarumlaut
```
Produces a long Hungarian umlaut accent over the following, as in ő.

```
\i
```
Produces a dotless i, as in 'ı'.

```
\j
```
Produces a dotless j, as in 'ȷ'.

```
\k
\capitalogonek
```
Produces a letter with ogonek, as in 'ǫ'. Not available in the OT1 encoding.

```
\r
\capitalring
```
Produces a ring accent, as in 'o̊'.

```
\t
\capitaltie
\newtie
\capitalnewtie
```
Produces a tie-after accent, as in 'oͦo'. The `\newtie` form is centered in its box.

```
\u
\capitalbreve
```
Produces a breve accent, as in 'ŏ'.

```
\underbar
```
Not exactly an accent, this produces a bar under the argument text. The argument is always processed in horizontal mode. The bar is always a fixed position under the baseline, thus crossing through descenders. See also `\underline` in Section 16.6 [Math miscellany], page 62.

```
\v
\capitalcaron
```
Produces a háček (check, caron) accent, as in 'ǒ'.

21.4 Non-English characters

Here are the basic LaTeX commands for inserting characters commonly used in languages other than English.

`\aa` `\AA`	å and Å.
`\ae` `\AE`	æ and Æ.
`\dh` `\DH`	Icelandic letter eth: ð and Ð.
`\dj` `\DJ`	Crossed d and D, a.k.a. capital and small letter d with stroke.
`\ij` `\IJ`	ij and IJ (except somewhat closer together than appears here).
`\l` `\L`	ł and Ł.
`\ng` `\NG`	Latin letter eng, also used in phonetics.
`\o` `\O`	ø and Ø.
`\oe` `\OE`	œ and Œ.
`\ss` `\SS`	ß and SS.
`\th` `\TH`	Icelandic letter thorn: þ and Þ.

21.5 `\rule`

Synopsis:

    \rule[raise]{width}{thickness}

The `\rule` command produces *rules*, that is, lines or rectangles. The arguments are:

raise How high to raise the rule (optional).

width The length of the rule (mandatory).

thickness The thickness of the rule (mandatory).

21.6 `\today`

The `\today` command produces today's date, in the format '*month dd, yyyy*'; for example, 'July 4, 1976'. It uses the predefined counters `\day`, `\month`, and `\year` (see Section 13.8 [\day \month \year], page 48) to do this. It is not updated as the program runs.

The `datetime` package, among others, can produce a wide variety of other date formats.

22 Splitting the input

A large document requires a lot of input. Rather than putting the whole input in a single large file, it's more efficient to split it into several smaller ones. Regardless of how many separate files you use, there is one that is the root file; it is the one whose name you type when you run LaTeX.

See Section 8.11 [filecontents], page 22, for an environment that allows bundling an external file to be created with the main document.

22.1 \include

Synopsis:

       \include{*file*}

If no \includeonly command is present, the \include command executes \clearpage to start a new page (see Section 10.2 [\clearpage], page 40), then reads *file*, then does another \clearpage.

Given an \includeonly command, the \include actions are only run if *file* is listed as an argument to \includeonly. See the next section.

The \include command may not appear in the preamble or in a file read by another \include command.

22.2 \includeonly

Synopsis:

       \includeonly{*file1,file2,...*}

The \includeonly command controls which files will be read by subsequent \include commands. The list of filenames is comma-separated. Each *file* must exactly match a filename specified in a \include command for the selection to be effective.

This command can only appear in the preamble.

22.3 \input

Synopsis:

       \input{*file*}

The \input command causes the specified *file* to be read and processed, as if its contents had been inserted in the current file at that point.

If *file* does not end in '.tex' (e.g., 'foo' or 'foo.bar'), it is first tried with that extension ('foo.tex' or 'foo.bar.tex'). If that is not found, the original *file* is tried ('foo' or 'foo.bar').

23 Front/back matter

23.1 Tables of contents

A table of contents is produced with the `\tableofcontents` command. You put the command right where you want the table of contents to go; LaTeX does the rest for you. A previous run must have generated a `.toc` file.

The `\tableofcontents` command produces a heading, but it does not automatically start a new page. If you want a new page after the table of contents, write a `\newpage` command after the `\tableofcontents` command.

The analogous commands `\listoffigures` and `\listoftables` produce a list of figures and a list of tables (from `.lof` and `.lot` files), respectively. Everything works exactly the same as for the table of contents.

The command `\nofiles` overrides these commands, and *prevents* any of these lists from being generated.

23.1.1 \addcontentsline

The `\addcontentsline{`*ext*`}{`*unit*`}{`*text*`}` command adds an entry to the specified list or table where:

ext	The extension of the file on which information is to be written, typically one of: `toc` (table of contents), `lof` (list of figures), or `lot` (list of tables).
unit	The name of the sectional unit being added, typically one of the following, matching the value of the *ext* argument:

	`toc`	The name of the sectional unit: `part`, `chapter`, `section`, `subsection`, `subsubsection`.
	`lof`	For the list of figures.
	`lot`	For the list of tables.
entry	The text of the entry.	

What is written to the `.ext` file is the command `\contentsline{`*unit*`}{`*name*`}`.

23.1.2 \addtocontents

The `\addtocontents{`*ext*`}{`*text*`}` command adds text (or formatting commands) directly to the `.ext` file that generates the table of contents or lists of figures or tables.

ext	The extension of the file on which information is to be written, typically one of: `toc` (table of contents), `lof` (list of figures), or `lot` (list of tables).
text	The text to be written.

23.2 Glossaries

The command `\makeglossary` enables creating glossaries.

The command `\glossary{text}` writes a glossary entry for *text* to an auxiliary file with the `.glo` extension.

Specifically, what gets written is the command `\glossaryentry{text}{pageno}`, where *pageno* is the current `\thepage` value.

The `glossary` package on CTAN provides support for fancier glossaries.

23.3 Indexes

The command `\makeindex` enables creating indexes. Put this in the preamble.

The command `\index{text}` writes an index entry for *text* to an auxiliary file with the `.idx` extension.

Specifically, what gets written is the command `\indexentry{text}{pageno}`, where *pageno* is the current `\thepage` value.

To generate a index entry for 'bar' that says 'See foo', use a vertical bar: `\index{bar|see{foo}}`. Use `seealso` instead of `see` to make a 'See also' entry.

The text 'See' is defined by the macro `\seename`, and 'See also' by the macro `\alsoname`. These can be redefined for other languages.

The generated `.idx` file is then sorted with an external command, usually either `makeindex` (http://mirror.ctan.org/indexing/makeindex) or (the multi-lingual) `xindy` (http://xindy.sourceforge.net). This results in a `.ind` file, which can then be read to typeset the index.

The index is usually generated with the `\printindex` command. This is defined in the `makeidx` package, so `\usepackage{makeidx}` needs to be in the preamble.

The rubber length `\indexspace` is inserted before each new letter in the printed index; its default value is '10pt plus5pt minus3pt'.

The `showidx` package causes each index entries to be shown in the margin on the page where the entry appears. This can help in preparing the index.

The `multind` package supports multiple indexes. See also the TeX FAQ entry on this topic, http://www.tex.ac.uk/cgi-bin/texfaq2html?label=multind.

24 Letters

You can use LaTeX to typeset letters, both personal and business. The `letter` document class is designed to make a number of letters at once, although you can make just one if you so desire.

Your `.tex` source file has the same minimum commands as the other document classes, i.e., you must have the following commands as a minimum:

```
\documentclass{letter}
\begin{document}
 ... letters ...
\end{document}
```

Each letter is a `letter` environment, whose argument is the name and address of the recipient. For example, you might have:

```
\begin{letter}{Mr. Joe Smith\\ 2345 Princess St.
    \\ Edinburgh, EH1 1AA}
  ...
\end{letter}
```

The letter itself begins with the `\opening` command. The text of the letter follows. It is typed as ordinary LaTeX input. Commands that make no sense in a letter, like `\chapter`, do not work. The letter closes with a `\closing` command.

After the `closing`, you can have additional material. The `\cc` command produces the usual "cc: ...". There's also a similar `\encl` command for a list of enclosures. With both these commands, use `\\` to separate the items.

These commands are used with the `letter` class.

24.1 \address{*return-address*}

The `\address` specifies the return address of a letter, as it should appear on the letter and the envelope. Separate lines of the address should be separated by `\\` commands.

If you do not make an `\address` declaration, then the letter will be formatted for copying onto your organization's standard letterhead. (See Chapter 2 [Overview], page 3, for details on your local implementation). If you give an `\address` declaration, then the letter will be formatted as a personal letter.

24.2 \cc

Synopsis:

```
\cc{name1\\name2}
```

Produce a list of *names* the letter was copied to. Each name is printed on a separate line.

24.3 \closing

Synopsis:

```
\closing{text}
```

A letter closes with a `\closing` command, for example,

```
\closing{Best Regards,}
```

24.4 \encl

Synopsis:

```
\encl{line1\\line2}
```

Declare a list of one more enclosures.

24.5 \location

```
\location{address}
```

This modifies your organization's standard address. This only appears if the **firstpage** pagestyle is selected.

24.6 \makelabels

```
\makelabels{number}
```

If you issue this command in the preamble, LATEX will create a sheet of address labels. This sheet will be output before the letters.

24.7 \name

```
\name{June Davenport}
```

Your name, used for printing on the envelope together with the return address.

24.8 \opening{text}

Synopsis:

```
\opening{text}
```

A letter begins with the **\opening** command. The mandatory argument, *text*, is whatever text you wish to start your letter. For instance:

```
\opening{Dear Joe,}
```

24.9 \ps

Use the **\ps** command to start a postscript in a letter, after **\closing**.

24.10 \signature{text}

Your name, as it should appear at the end of the letter underneath the space for your signature. \\ starts a new line within *text* as usual.

24.11 \startbreaks

```
\startbreaks
```

Used after a **\stopbreaks** command to allow page breaks again.

24.12 \stopbreaks

\stopbreaks

Inhibit page breaks until a \startbreaks command occurs.

24.13 \telephone

\telephone{number}

This is your telephone number. This only appears if the firstpage pagestyle is selected.

25 Terminal input/output

25.1 \typein[*cmd*]{*msg*}

Synopsis:

> \typein[*cmd*]{*msg*}

\typein prints *msg* on the terminal and causes LaTeX to stop and wait for you to type a line of input, ending with return. If the optional *cmd* argument is omitted, the typed input is processed as if it had been included in the input file in place of the \typein command. If the *cmd* argument is present, it must be a command name. This command name is then defined or redefined to be the typed input.

25.2 \typeout{*msg*}

Synopsis:

> \typeout{*msg*}

Prints msg on the terminal and in the log file. Commands in msg that are defined with \newcommand or \renewcommand (among others) are replaced by their definitions before being printed.

LaTeX's usual rules for treating multiple spaces as a single space and ignoring spaces after a command name apply to msg. A \space command in msg causes a single space to be printed, independent of surrounding spaces. A ^^J in msg prints a newline.

26 Command line

The input file specification indicates the file to be formatted; TeX uses `.tex` as a default file extension. If you omit the input file entirely, TeX accepts input from the terminal. You can also specify arbitrary LaTeX input by starting with a backslash. For example, this processes `foo.tex` without pausing after every error:

```
latex '\nonstopmode\input foo.tex'
```

With many, but not all, implementations, command-line options can also be specified in the usual Unix way, starting with '-' or '--'. For a list of those options, try '`latex --help`'.

If LaTeX stops in the middle of the document and gives you a '`*`' prompt, it is waiting for input. You can type `\stop` (and return) and it will prematurely end the document.

See Section 2.3 [TeX engines], page 4, for other system commands invoking LaTeX.

Appendix A Document templates

Although not reference material, perhaps these document templates will be useful. Additional template resources are listed at `http://tug.org/interest.html#latextemplates`.

A.1 beamer template

The `beamer` class creates presentation slides. It has a vast array of features, but here is a basic template:

```
\documentclass{beamer}

\title{Beamer Class template}
\author{Alex Author}
\date{July 31, 2007}

\begin{document}

\maketitle

% without [fragile], any {verbatim} code gets mysterious errors.
\begin{frame}[fragile]
 \frametitle{First Slide}

\begin{verbatim}
  This is \verbatim!
\end{verbatim}

\end{frame}

\end{document}
```

One web resource for this: `http://robjhyndman.com/hyndsight/beamer/`.

A.2 book template

```
\documentclass{book}
\title{Book Class Template}
\author{Alex Author}

\begin{document}
\maketitle

\chapter{First}
Some text.

\chapter{Second}
Some other text.
```

```
\section{A subtopic}
The end.
\end{document}
```

A.3 tugboat template

TUGboat is the journal of the TeX Users Group, `http://tug.org/TUGboat`.

```
\documentclass{ltugboat}
\usepackage{graphicx}
\usepackage{ifpdf}
\ifpdf
\usepackage[breaklinks,hidelinks]{hyperref}
\else
\usepackage{url}
\fi

\title{Example \TUB\ article}

% repeat info for each author.
\author{First Last}
\address{Street Address \\ Town, Postal \\ Country}
\netaddress{user (at) example dot org}
\personalURL{http://example.org/~user/}

\begin{document}

\maketitle

\begin{abstract}
This is an example article for \TUB{}.
\end{abstract}

\section{Introduction}

This is an example article for \TUB, from
\url{http://tug.org/TUGboat/location.html}.

We recommend the \texttt{graphicx} package for image inclusions, and the
\texttt{hyperref} package for active urls in the \acro{PDF} output.
Nowadays \TUB\ is produced using \acro{PDF} files exclusively.

The \texttt{ltugboat} class provides these abbreviations and many more:

% verbatim blocks are often better in \small
\begin{verbatim}[\small]
\AllTeX \AMS \AmS \AmSLaTeX \AmSTeX \aw \AW
\BibTeX \CTAN \DTD \HTML
```

```
\ISBN \ISSN \LaTeXe
\Mc \mf \MFB \mtex \PCTeX \pcTeX
\PiC \PiCTeX \plain \POBox \PS
\SC \SGML \SliTeX \TANGLE \TB \TP
\TUB \TUG \tug
\UG \UNIX \VAX \XeT \WEB \WEAVE

\Dash \dash \vellipsis \bull \cents \Dag
\careof \thinskip

\acro{FRED} -> {\small[er] fred}  % please use!
\cs{fred}   -> \fred
\env{fred}  -> \begin{fred}
\meta{fred} -> <fred>
\nth{n}     -> 1st, 2nd, ...
\sfrac{3/4} -> 3/4
\booktitle{Book of Fred}
\end{verbatim}

For more information, see the ltubguid document at:
\url{http://mirror.ctan.org/macros/latex/contrib/tugboat}
(we recommend using \verb|mirror.ctan.org| for \CTAN\ references).

Email \verb|tugboat@tug.org| if problems or questions.

\bibliographystyle{plain}  % we recommend the plain bibliography style
\nocite{book-minimal}      % just making the bibliography non-empty
\bibliography{xampl}       % xampl.bib comes with BibTeX

\makesignature
\end{document}
```

Concept Index

Command Index